JUDE,
THE EPISTLE

A Commentary for Today

First in the "Commentary for Today" Series

All Scripture is taken from the Authorized King James Bible

Definitions were taken from the Strong's Concordance, unless otherwise stated.

In the face of pressure to dilute pure Christian doctrine, Jude's aim for his readers were to stand firm and earnestly contend for the faith. May you and I do likewise.

Copyright 2016

By: Matthew B. Jones

Apology-

In hopes to attract the average Christian to connect deeper in their faith and love for the Savior, I have written this Commentary. My purpose was not to replace another man's work on Jude with my own, but to add to the wealth of knowledge that is out there for one's learning.

I began this adventure by preaching through the little book of Jude. The deep study I joyfully borne while preparing my messages brought me to realize how much the book of Jude is very relevant for you and I today.

I hope that you will not only enjoy this book but retain and use what knowledge you may obtain from it.

May God, bless you in your ministry for Him.

Your Brother in Christ,
Matthew B. Jones

All **bold** text is of the book of Jude.

All ***bold and italicized*** text is of other Scripture references.

All <u>underlined</u> text are words that are being defined.

All *italicized* text are the definitions of the words underlined.

OUTLINE

Jude's Greeting-*Verses 1-2*

Jude's Reason for Writing-*Verses 3-4*

Jude's Warnings Regarding False Teachers, Beliefs, and Practices-*Verses 5-16*

Jude's Appeal to Avoid Error and Remain Faithful to Christ-*Verses 17-23*

Jude's Doxology: Glory to God through Jesus Christ-*Verses 24-25*

About the Book:

The Author- Jude, pronounced Judah- in Hebrew and Judas- in Greek.

The First Question we must ask ourselves is who was Jude? It is supposed that this Jude is the half-brother of Christ our Lord. The Gospel of Matthew names Jude as so. Look at Matthew 13:55-*Is not this the carpenter's son? Is not his mother called Mary? And his brethren, James and Joses, and Simon, and Judas?*

Also, we see this in the Gospel of Mark Chapter 6:3-*Is not this the carpenter, the son of Mary, the brother of James, and Joses, and of Judah and Simon? And are not his sisters here with us? And they were offended at him.*

At first, we are told that Jude did not believe his half-brother, Jesus was the Messiah. We see this in the Gospel of John 7: 3-5-*His brethren therefore said unto him, depart hence, and go into Judaea, that thy disciples also may see the works that thou doest. For there is no man that doeth any thing in secret, and he himself seeketh to be known openly. If thou do these things, shew thyself to the world. For neither did his brethren believe in him.*

We find out that something happened from that time to the resurrection of Christ, that His brothers now believe in Him as Lord. Look at what the book of Acts says: 1:14-*These all continued with one accord in prayer and supplication, with the women, and Mary the mother of Jesus, and with his brethren.* We see Jude along with his other brothers gathered with the Apostles.

So, we see that to begin with, Jude was an unbeliever, as seen in (John 7:3,5), but after the resurrection he was now among the apostles and others, (Acts 1:14).

The second question that we should ask is, "Why was the book of Jude written?" It was said that doctrinal error was creeping into the early church. Jude is the only New Testament book devoted exclusively to confronting "apostasy" meaning *the defection from the true, biblical faith.* Jude mentions this in verses 3 and 17.

He called for a discernment on the part of the church and a rigorous defense of biblical truth. Another thing to note is that Jude is filled with Old Testament illustrations, including:

A.   The Exodus of the children of Israel from Egypt-verse 5

B.   Satan's Rebellion-verse 6
C.   The destruction of the cities of Sodom and Gomorrah-verse 7
D.   The death of Moses-verse 9
E.   The manner of Cain-verse 11
F.   The mistake of Balaam-verse. 11
G.   The opposition of Korah-verse 11
H.   The preaching of Enoch-verses 14,15

Jude 1-**Jude, the servant of Jesus Christ, and brother of James, to them that are sanctified by God the Father, and preserved in Jesus Christ, and called:**

Jude, the servant of Jesus Christ- We know that this was Jude, the half-brother of our Lord Jesus Christ. The word <u>servant</u> means *bond servant or even a slave*. Jude was also the brother of James, Author of the book of James, who was also the pastor of the church of Jerusalem.

Why did Jude refer to himself as a servant? Why not brother, or half-brother? It's possible that others already knew who he was concerning his physical relationship with Christ. Better yet, it's even more possible that he understood that the important thing isn't being physically related to the Lord, but to be spiritually related. That's the difference between heaven and hell. You and I need to know this also. Our relation to who our parents are, will never decide whether you spend eternity in heaven, its only through the spiritual relationship you have with Christ. That's the difference.

To them- Who was "them" that Jude was referring to? I want us to look closely here; there are three 'specifics' whom he was speaking of:

1. The Sanctified-those who are set apart for sacred services.

2. The Preserved- those kept from evil.

3. The Called- those who are established or ordained.

Let's take a deeper look at who these three specific groups were that Jude penned this letter to.

Sanctified by God the Father- <u>Sanctified</u> means *set apart for sacred services.* Who was Jude speaking of in this verse? Look with me in; John 17:17 & 19- ***Sanctify them through thy truth: thy word is truth. And for their sakes I sanctify myself, that they also might be sanctified through the truth.***

Jude was speaking to the church. Christians, how are we sanctified? In both verses, it says ***"through thy truth."*** The truth is God's word. We are sanctified through God's word, by God's word. The more you read God's word, and apply His word, it cleanses us. How? by His washing us with His word, therefore, we are sanctified through the truth.

We see this principle in Ephesians 5:25-26, ***Husbands, love your wives, even as Christ also loved the church, and gave himself for it, that he*** *might sanctify and cleanse it with the washing of water by the word.* So, as the body of believers, being the Church, Christ sanctifies us, (the body, the Church) and cleanses it with the washing of water by the word.

And Preserved in Jesus Christ- Preserved means *kept from evil.* Look with me in John 17:15-*I pray not that thou shouldest take them out of the world, but that thou shouldest keep them from the evil.* This is Christ's prayer for His disciples the night of His betrayal. He asked not for God to take them (his disciples) out of this world but to keep them from evil while in this world. Therefore, when a person gets saved, they're not taken straight to heaven. No, we have a job to do here, while performing that job we are preserved by God.

Look with me in 2 Timothy 4:18-*and the Lord shall deliver me from every evil work, and will preserve me unto his heavenly kingdom....* There's that word again. Preserve. Paul was saying that he stayed busy working for God while God preserved him. The same goes with us. You stay busy, don't give up, don't quit; only quit worrying about how you're going to make it. Just know that God is there and He will preserve you. Don't Quit!

Look at what Christ said in John 10:28-30, *And I give unto them eternal life; and they shall never perish, neither shall any man pluck them out of my hand. My Father, which gave them me, is greater than all; and no man is able to pluck them out of my Father's hand. I and my Father are one.*

Of course, this doesn't mean that we will always have it easy, that there will be no heartaches. No, of course not. But it does mean that you will never lose your salvation, you will always have a place in heaven to call home. No one can take that away from you. It's yours from now on. You are preserved, protected by God.

And called- Called means *appointed, ordained or established.* In 1 Peter 2:9 God said, *But ye are a chosen generation a royal priesthood, an holy nation, a peculiar people, that ye should show forth the praises of him who hath called you out of darkness into his marvelous light.*

What does it mean to be called? First, we've been called out of darkness. Remember, before you were saved, you were in darkness. The darkness is the darkness of sin. But now we have been called out of darkness and into His marvelous light. We can see the way, His way, no more stumbling and feeling around.

It says in 1 Thessalonians 2:12-*That ye would walk worthy of God, who hath called you unto his kingdom and glory*. Here we are called unto his kingdom and glory, though as of now we're still on this earth but you and I have been invited or appointed to meet God at His home, or kingdom in heaven, where also His glory appears.

Can you imagine one day, no more heartaches, perfect vision, a perfect body. No more pain, or suffering. No more tears to flow down our cheeks. For they will be wiped away.

Look at 2 Timothy 1:9-*Who hath saved us, and called us with a holy calling, not according to our works, but according to his own purpose and grace, which was given us in Christ Jesus before the world began.* It's a <u>holy</u> calling meaning *hallowed; consecrated or set apart for sacred use, or the service of worship of our God.*

Before the world began, God had planned for us to be called with a holy calling, for the service and worship of God. I believe that God's will is that all come to repentance, and with that, all have been called, but not all choose to come. The choice is left to you. You must decide to accept or reject Christ's call.

It says in Philippians 3:14-*I press toward the mark for the prize of the high calling of God in Christ Jesus.* We should see the calling of God as it is, the prize of an incorruptible crown, in an incorruptible heaven. It's a joy to serve God, not a burden, not dreaded. Though, like a race, there will be hills to struggle up, there will be dry dusty land to cross over, but the reward is eternal, not temporal. If you think that the prize of a home in heaven is not worth it, then your serving the wrong god.

We see that God's call has a fourfold emphasis:

1. He calls men everywhere to come out of darkness into the light, His light.

2. All Christians are called to His kingdom and Glory. Service to Him.

3. God calls us with a holy calling, it's a specific sphere of service or ministry.

4. It's a high calling. It is a joy to serve the Lord.

Let's summarize the text; Yes, Jude was speaking to a very specific group of people in his epistle

He was speaking to:

1. The Sanctified-Christians whose lives have been washed by the washing of water by the word. They have set themselves apart for God's work.

2. The preserved- means kept from evil, while we stay busy for God, He preserves us (keeps us from evil.) Not saying that nothing bad will ever happen to us, but, evil will not hurt us nor endanger us. We are preserved by the fact that we don't go looking for evil, get caught up in the latest evil. Preserved because we are too busy serving and are satisfied in His work

3. The Called- appointed or established.

We've seen in this verse that Jude was written for a specific group of people. A special group, known by God. That group is called the church. The church is a body of believers called Christians. Today, are you a Christian? Only you can know for sure. Why not settle it and bring your cares to Jesus? Before the world began God called you. The question is, how will you answer?

Jude 2-Mercy unto you, and peace, and love, be multiplied.

Mercy unto you, and peace, and love- Ok, now we know that this Epistle was written to the early Christians. We gathered that from verse one. Now we see Jude greeting us with a three-fold blessing;

1. Mercy- The Greek word is eleos meaning, *pity or compassion.*

2. Peace- The Greek word is Eirene meaning, *peace of mind.*

3. Love- The Greek word is agape meaning, *benevolence, good will.*

We can trace these blessings back to the Trinity. Look with me;

1. **Mercy-** Psalm 136:26-*O give thanks unto the God of heaven: for his mercy endureth for ever.* Our mercy comes from the Father.
2. **Peace-** Romans 14:17-*for the kingdom of God is not meat and drink, but righteousness, and peace, and joy in the Holy Ghost.* Our peace comes from the Holy Ghost.
3. **Love-** Romans 8:35-*Who shall separate us from the love of Christ? Shall tribulation, or distress, or persecution, or famine, or nakedness, or peril, or sword?* Our love comes from the Lord.

Also, don't forget the last statement in this verse;

Be multiplied- Whether you realize it today, you are overflowing with mercy, with peace, and with love. We have a Father who continues to show us these blessings daily, all the while we are undeserving of any of them.

Jude 3-**Beloved, when I gave all diligence to write unto you of the common salvation, it was needful for me to write unto you, and exhort you that ye should earnestly contend for the faith which was once delivered unto the saints.**

Beloved- I like this word, <u>Beloved.</u> This word means *greatly loved or dear to the heart.* Jude wasn't writing to strangers, but those who are dear to his heart. Today this epistle is still capable of speaking to our hearts. As you continue to read and study Jude, allow God, through the Holy Spirit, to speak to you through His word.

Just as the readers of the original letter from Jude were his beloved, today, you are the beloved of God. You are greatly loved. Let's look on;

When I gave all diligence to write unto you of the common salvation- <u>Diligence</u> means *care; heed; steady application in business of any kind.* <u>Common</u> means *to have a joint right with others in common ground.* There is nothing common or ordinary about our salvation. This common speaks of salvation being the same for you as it is for me. Not being ordinary. Our salvation isn't ordinary. Special, yes! Precious, yes! Priceless, yes! But, it is also common or equal for each of us.

Allow me to explain to you a little bit about this '**common salvation.**'

In Isaiah 45:17-***But Israel shall be saved in the LORD with an everlasting salvation;*** Isaiah said in this verse that it's an everlasting salvation. Once we obtain it, it's ours for life, life everlasting. How did we get this salvation?

It says in Isaiah 45:22- ***Look unto me, and be ye saved, all the ends of the earth: for I am God, and there is none else.*** This tells me that I couldn't look to myself and be saved, I must look to God for my salvation.

Today, anyone who desires redemption must look unto God for salvation, it's unavailable anywhere else. Isaiah said *for **I am God, and there is none else.*** Salvation comes only from God.

Look at Acts 4:12-***Neither is there salvation in any other: for there is none other name under heaven given among men, whereby we must be saved.*** So, this "**common salvation**" is special in the fact that it's an everlasting salvation, it's given by faith; ***look unto me***; and it only comes from Christ.

It was needful for me to write unto you, and exhort you- That word <u>exhort</u> means *to advise; to caution; to warn.* Jude had something very important to discuss with his friends. It was needful to write, and not only to write, but also to exhort, meaning he had something to advise them or warn them about.

Jude was saying I have something important to discuss with you.

You know, when we read God's word, we need to read it like it is something important. Its more than a book…It's the word of God, given unto us by our heavenly Father. We need to quit reading it and thinking of it like it was some sort of novel. The Bible holds the key to everlasting freedom.

That ye should earnestly contend for the faith- Contend means *to defend or preserve*; so, he was asking them to be a defender or a preserver. For what? the faith. Did you realize that as a Christian you have a duty? That duty is to be a defender for the faith.

Look at Philippians 1:27-*Only let your conversation be as it becometh the gospel of Christ: that whether I come and see you, or else be absent, I may hear of your affairs, that ye stand fast in one spirit, with one mind striving together for the faith of the gospel;*

That word strive means the same as contend. We need to band together as Christians and be defenders; preservers for the faith. There needs to be a union within the local church. Not only that but also within the body of Christ, meaning all churches.

In 1 Thessalonians 2:2 Paul spoke of the suffering that they went through at Philippi. Nevertheless, he said, *we were bold in our God to speak unto you the gospel….* They were bold in their God to speak what? The gospel of God, even though there was much contention.

Look at 1 Timothy 1:18-*That thou mightest war a good warfare…* Now, look at verse 19-*Holding faith.* Why? *Which some having put away, concerning faith have made shipwreck:*

Some have ruined their lives because they did not *hold the faith*. Because of this everything was lost…everything. You and I have too much to lose. We are to stand strong and as Paul, *holding the faith*, that's our life, our future.

The Bible says in 1 Timothy 6:12-*Fight the good fight of faith, lay hold on eternal life, where unto thou art also called, and hast professed a good profession before many witnesses.* Then at the end of Paul's life he said in 2 Timothy 4:7-*I have fought a good fight, I have finished my course, I have kept the faith:*

How is your faith today? Think about it. What do you worry about, what are your weaknesses? Have you kept your faith?

Which was once delivered unto the saints- What was delivered unto the saints? The gospel. The Bible says in 1 Cor. 15:3-*For I delivered unto you first of all that which I also received, how that Christ died for our sins according to the Scriptures;* Then in Galatians 2:5-...*that the truth of the gospel might continue with you.* How else will our posterity know God? How else will they get saved? It is now on us to deliver the gospel, the gospel that we defend and protect.

So, Jude said in verse 3, he was writing unto us of our unique salvation though common in the fact that to each of us, there is an equal portion given. He warned us that we need to strive to be preservers and defenders, not of the faith but for the faith. The faith of our fathers, this is that saving faith that can change your eternal destiny. How are you doing as a defender for the faith? Do you need a little work at it?

Jude 4-**For there are certain men crept in unawares, who were before of old ordained to this condemnation, ungodly men, turning the grace of our God into lasciviousness, and denying the only Lord God, and our Lord Jesus Christ.**

For there are certain men crept in unawares- We have an illustration of this in Acts 15:24-*Forasmuch as we have heard, that certain which went out from us have troubled you with words, subverting your souls, saying, ye must be circumcised, and keep the law: to whom we gave no such commandment.*

You must realize that these types of people, the so-called church goers, are everywhere. They blend in with Christians and deceive most ignorant believers.

That is why we must study, we must constantly pray, we must constantly know what is going on within our church so that if it creeps into the local assembly, we can as Barney Fife would say, "nip it in the bud." That's our job as Christians, to be defenders, preservers, as is stated in the previous verse.

This is also seen in Galatians 2:4-*...who came in privily to spy out our liberty...that they might bring us into bondage.* What was their sole purpose? to bring them into bondage.

Paul told us in Ephesians. 4:14-*that we henceforth be no more children....* We are not to flip flop on our standards, convictions or principles. We're not to get caught up in the latest rage. There are those out there that want to deceive you and that's it. When we go off on tangents as most Christians do, we forget the big picture; that would be how should a Christian act.

Peter warned us of this in 2 Peter 2:1- *But there were false prophets, also among the people, even as there shall be false teachers among you, who privily shall bring in damnable heresies, even denying the Lord that brought them, and bring upon themselves swift destruction.* There are several passages that speaks of this issue. We must watch!

Who were before of old ordained to this condemnation- These are men and women that flat out rejected the truth. In doing so, they have become apostates who are now trying to destroy the faith of others. These people are not your friends; they want to hurt you and your church.

Ungodly men- Who are these men and what is their agenda? It says in the book of Psalms 1:1-*blessed is the man that walketh not in the* *counsel of the ungodly, nor standeth in the way of sinners, nor sitters in the seat of the scornful.*

Look, we don't get our counsel from the ungodly. We don't ask them their advice about the things of God. Look at what Peter said in 2 Peter 2:5-7-*...bringing in the flood upon the world of the ungodly. ...making them an example unto those that after should live ungodly. But the heavens and the earth, which are now, by the same word are kept in store, reserved unto fire against the day of judgment and perdition of ungodly men.*

One-day God is going to judge these ungodly men, and we shouldn't interfere with His judgment but allow Him to handle it. We get in God's way when we try to handle the wicked ourselves.

Turning the grace of our God into lasciviousness- Lasciviousness *irregular indulgence of animal desires; lustfulness.* Is this how we should live? NO!! Look at Romans 6:1,2- *What shall we say then? Shall we continue in sin, that grace may abound? God forbid. How shall we, that are dead to sin, live any longer therein?*

Look with me also at Titus 2:11,12-*For the grace of God that bringeth salvation hath appeared to all men, teaching us that, denying ungodliness and worldly lusts, we should live soberly, righteously, and godly, in this present world;*

Now let's go to 2 Peter 2:10-*But chiefly them that walk after the flesh in the lusts of uncleanness, and despise government. Presumptuous are they, self-willed, they are not afraid to speak evil of dignities.*

These are perverted men, not Christians, nowhere near being Christians. Their hearts have been seared with a hot iron, along with their conscience. You and I need to stay clear of these types of people.

And denying- Titus 1:15,16-*...but in works they deny him....* You and I must be careful that our works are not of such that will deny God, or Christ's work on the cross. Folks this is serious. This isn't a game; we don't get second chances at life.

Now look at 2 Peter 2:1-*But there were false prophets also among the people, even as there shall be false teachers among you, who privily shall bring in damnable heresies, even denying the Lord that bought them, and bring upon themselves swift destruction.*

Here in Peter, he is referring to when Israel had to contend with false prophets among them. Saying that now we need to be on the lookout for false teachers, teaching heresies, and denying our Lord. We have an urgent job to do in identifying the false teachers and straightening out the heresies that they've sown.

The only Lord God, and our Lord Jesus Christ- Who are they denying? The ONLY Lord God, and Lord Jesus Christ.

John 17:3-*And this is life eternal, that they might know thee the only true God, and Jesus Christ, whom thou hast sent.*

Rev. 15:4- *who shall not fear thee, O Lord, and Glorify thy name?*

This tells me that everyone shall one day fear the Lord- whether they like it or not, God will be feared.

In review of verse four we see that there will be those that will sneak in to add or take away from the gospel. These apostates have long rejected Christ and salvation, and their hearts have hardened. These people are ungodly; they have no business being in authority in our church. Jude says that they turn God's grace into sexual perversion! How dare we socialize with them. They are cults, perverts, and blasphemers. They hate laws, the government, and God. They deny God's word and Christ's work on the cross while knowing that Christ only, deserves the praise and honor.

Jude 5-**I will therefore put you in remembrance, though ye once knew this, how that the Lord, having saved the people out of the land of Egypt, afterward destroyed them that believed not.**

I will therefore put you in remembrance, though ye once knew this- God knows that we often forget our past. He's given us the Old Testament to study for examples so that we can remember the cause and the effects of what happened with Israel. This is for our benefit.

It says this in Romans 15:4-*For whatsoever things were written afore time were written for our learning, that we through patience and comfort of the Scriptures might have hope.*

We read, we learn, we remember, this is for our advantage. All too often, the reason we get ourselves into so much hot water with the Lord is that we don't ever remember that the sins we continue to toy with are the ones that always get us into trouble. I know that sounds simple, but it's true.

You and I need to realize that God is giving us these examples so that we don't go down the same path of sin as they did, though usually, we neglect God's warning, and end up in the same situation as the Hebrews did.

Look at 1 Cor. 10:11-*Now all these things happened unto them for examples: and they are written for our admonition, upon whom the ends of the world are come.* That word admonition means *gentle reproof; counseling against a fault.* It's time that we take God's admonition and learn from others' mistakes.

Why is it that we are so hard headed that we must fail on our own before we realize that what we are doing is wrong? God has given us such wonderful examples to follow, why can't we follow them? Why does it always seem so hard?

How that the Lord, having saved the people out of the land of Egypt, afterward destroyed them that believed not- The rest of the verse here, Jude gave us an example from the Old Testament. Numbers 14:20-37-*And the LORD said, I have pardoned according to thy word: But as truly as I live, all the earth shall be filled with the glory of the LORD. Because all those men which have seen my glory, and my miracles, which I did in Egypt and in the wilderness, and have tempted me now these ten times, and have not hearkened to my voice; Surely they shall not see the land which I sware unto their fathers, neither shall any of them that provoked me see it: But my servant Caleb, because he had another spirit with him, and hath followed me* *fully, him will I bring into the land where into he went; and his seed shall possess it. (Now the Amalekites and the Canaanites dwelt in the valley.) To morrow turn you, and get you into the wilderness by the way of the Red Sea. And the LORD spake unto Moses and unto Aaron, saying, How long shall I bear with this evil congregation, which murmur against me? I have heard the murmurings of the children of Israel, which they murmur against me. Say unto them, As truly as I live, saith the LORD, as ye have spoken in mine ears, so will I do to you: Your carcasses shall fall in this wilderness; and all that were numbered of you, according to your whole number, from twenty years old and upward, which have murmured against me, Doubtless ye shall not come into the land, concerning which I share to make you dwell therein, save Caleb the son of Jephunneh, and Joshua the son of Nun. But your little ones, which ye said should be a prey, them will I bring in, and they shall know the land which ye have despised. But as for you, your carcasses, they shall fall in this wilderness. And your children shall wander in the wilderness forty years, and bear your whoredoms, until your carcasses be wasted in the wilderness. After the number of the days in which ye searched the land, even forty days, each day for a year, shall ye bear your iniquities, even forty years, and ye shall know my breach of promise. I the LORD have said, I will surely do it unto all this evil congregation, that are gathered together against me: in this wilderness they shall be consumed, and there they shall die. And the men, which Moses sent to search the land, who returned, and made all the congregation to murmur against him, by bringing up a slander upon the land, Even those men that did bring up the evil report upon the land, died by the plague before the Lord.*

These chosen people of the Lord, they would not harken to God's voice. They would not by faith accept God at His word. They murmured constantly, they saw the glory of God, they saw the mighty works done in Egypt. They looked on as God's mighty hand stretched forth to deliver the plagues unto Egypt while His other hand protected them in the land of Goshen. Then when Pharaoh kicked them out of Egypt, they crossed the Red Sea and saw the walls of water congealed like Jell-O.

Once on the other side of the Red Sea, they gave God a victory song, and danced before Him giving Him praises.

But, that was short lived. Time and time again, they complained to God about everything. Till finally God had enough. "No more!" He cried out.

God's wrath was poured out on the same congregation that He once delivered out of the land of Egypt.

We must remember that no one can presume upon past mercies that they are now out of danger. That God in sparing us, has somehow withdrawn His hand of vengeance upon us, regardless of our lifestyle or sins. Though God may indeed have greatly invested in you, His righteousness remains forever; His Wrath is still poured out upon the wicked. He will still condemn; He will still be feared.

God will not share His glory with anyone! Nor will He be mocked. All the Israelites' sins can be summed up into one word: unbelief.

So, we see in verse 5, that it complements verse 4. Showing us that these **"certain men, before of old ordain"** though they caused much confusion, they will not get away with it. God will judge them.

Just like you and me. We must remember that God will not be mocked, He will judge us if the need arises. That's why it's important to live godly lives, clean lives, pure lives, holy before a Holy God.

If we've gotten anything from verse five, it's that we must keep our selves pure, remember we serve a great God, but one that's due respect. God is worthy of our utmost sincere gratitude. Remember that it was complaining that got the Israelites into so much trouble. We complain when we don't believe that God is in control. We must never allow that to continue in our life. When you catch yourself complaining, cut it off, quickly. Don't allow yourself to be consumed with such vulgar thoughts.

Remember we serve a powerful God. One who loves us, but, also one who will punish us when He sees fit.

Jude 6-**And the angels which kept not their first estate, but left their own habitation, he hath reserved in everlasting chains under darkness unto the judgment of the great day.**

We looked in verse five at the illustration of the children of Israel whom God judged. God condemned thousands of His people due to their unbelief and murmuring. This was God's chosen people, handpicked by God Himself. As we now know, they weren't above condemnation, and now Jude is giving us the example of the fallen angels.

And the angels which kept not their first estate- Ok, allow me to ask a couple of questions here. First, who are these Angels? they are the fallen angels. Secondly, how do we know this? because it says they "**kept not their first estate.**"

What does that term mean? first- *means the rank or honor that they had in heaven.* Estate *means principality or territory which was heaven.* When these angels aligned themselves with Satan, their rank and pre-eminence they did not keep, though originally it was assigned to them by God.

They once enjoyed the goodness of God and His bountiful blessings. But once Satan rebelled, these approximately one third of the angels rebelled with him. They believed Satan's lie, that he should be equal with God. To be cast from heaven was not their final judgment, but only part of it. The rest of their judgment is coming at The Great Judgment.

These are the same fallen angels that Paul spoke of in Ephesians 6:12-*For we wrestle not against flesh and blood, but against principalities, against powers, against the rulers of the darkness of this world, against spiritual wickedness in high places.*

Paul spoke here of an enemy, not of one we can see and feel, but of the invisible enemy that makes war with us. Though we can't see the war, we are still in it. It's a spiritual warfare. These fallen angels attack us from every side, that's why we are told about the armor of God. That's why it's important to maintain your spiritual defense.

Your mind is a treasure that the enemy desires to take. But, you and I must fight to maintain our pure thoughts, our godly habits. It's a constant spiritual battle, but God has given us the weapons that are needed to win. We don't have to be a casualty.

But left their own habitation- Originally, they were heavenly beings, surrounding the heavenly throne, able to freely see and speak to God, to worship Him. Now what is their habitation but a wasteland, endless, only altering when the Great Judgment Day comes, then begins their eternal torment in the Lake of Fire.

He hath reserved in everlasting chains under darkness unto the judgment of the great day- We know from other passages that these 'everlasting chains' bind them not in a pit of hell, for at this very moment they constantly seek to hinder God's soldiers from serving Him. But these chains nevertheless, bind them to a coming judgment, with which they cannot break forth from.

Matthew 8:29-*and, behold, they cried out, saying, What have we to do with thee, Jesus, thou Son of God? Art thou come hither to torment us before the time?* You see, they know that there will be a final judgment, and when they saw the Son of God, they feared that the judgment was coming early.

Then we see the final destruction of Satan and these fallen angels in Revelation 20:10-*And the devil that deceived them was cast into the lake of fire and brimstone, where the beast and the false prophet are, and shall be tormented day and night for ever and ever.* That will be the day of judgment for these fallen angels, they will finally get what has been so long coming to them.

Let's look at Matthew 25:41-*then shall he say also unto them on the left hand depart from me, ye cursed, into everlasting fire, prepared for the devil and his angels:*

This verse tells me two things. First, that Satan and his angels will have their day. Secondly, that the eternal punishment of hell wasn't meant for human beings. It was created originally for Satan and his condemned angels. We know this from what Christ said in Matthew 25:41-...*Depart from me, ye cursed, into everlasting fire, prepared for the devil and his angels.* But due to unbelief and rejecting the blood of Christ, it is now being used to house the unregenerate, those who willfully choose to reject God.

2 Peter 2:4-*For if God spared not the angels that sinned, but cast them down to hell, and delivered them into chains of darkness, to be reserved unto judgment;* Peter was telling us the same thing that Jude was telling us, God has mercy, but, we don't abuse that mercy. The angels didn't get away with sin, neither shall mankind.

Jude 7-**Even as Sodom and Gomorrah, and the cities about them in like manner, giving themselves over to fornication, and going after strange flesh, are set forth for an example, suffering the vengeance of eternal fire.**

Even as Sodom and Gomorrah, and the cities about them in like manner- My first question is why are these two cities named? I believe that in order to answer this question, we must know a little about these two cities.

Sodom and Gomorrah are first mentioned in Genesis 10:19, the verse refers to the land that the Canaanites possessed.

In Genesis 13:10-*And Lot lifted up his eyes, and beheld all the plain of Jordan, that it was well watered every where, before the LORD destroyed Sodom and Gomorrah, even as the garden of the LORD, like the land of Egypt, as thou comest unto Zoar.* Could you imagine a land that the Bible refers to as being like unto the garden of the LORD? it must have been a beautiful sight to see.

Lot was a herdsman, so seeing this land as the Bible says that it was well-watered. I would think that it would have been perfect for him and his occupation.

Here is an interesting note concerning Sodom; it is mentioned 47 times in the Bible. In all the Bible, not one verse speaks of Sodom and Gomorrah in a good way. Even in this verse, after describing it as being like the garden of the LORD, God interjects that small phrase (*before the LORD destroyed Sodom and Gomorrah*) What a statement about these two cities! What was so bad about these cities that it is mentioned so many times and always in a negative way?

Giving themselves over to fornication- Fornication has four different meanings. Firsts it means-*The incontinence (lack of self-control) or lewdness of unmarried persons, male or female; also, the criminal conversation of a married man with an unmarried woman.*

Secondly it means, *Adultery.* A good biblical example of this is in Matthew chapter 5. Third we have *Incest.* A biblical example of this is found in 1 Corinthians chapter 5. The forth one is Idolatry. This is *a forsaking of the true God, and worshipping of idols.* A good biblical example of this is found in 2 Chronicles chapter 21 and Revelation chapter 19.

I personally believe that all four of these types of acts and more were being performed in Sodom. Let's look at this more closely. Look at Genesis

19:4-8-*But before they lay down, the men of the city, even the men of Sodom, compasseth the house round, both old and young, all the people from every quarter: and they called unto Lot, and said unto him, where are the men which came in to thee this night? Bring them out unto us, that we may know them. And Lot went out at the door unto them, and shut the door after him. And said, I pray you brethren do not so wickedly. Behold now, I have two daughters which have not known man; let me, I pray you, bring them out unto you, and do ye to them as is good in your eyes: only unto these men do nothing; for therefore came they under the shadow of my roof.*

Lot brings two angels into his home to stay the night. That evening the men of the city surrounded his house and demanded him to bring the two 'men' out so they might have sexual actions with them. The term know means in the Hebrew for this verse, *to know a person carnally, of sexual intercourse, man subject and object of sodomy.* This shows the lack of self-control, and the obsession of lewdness. Men wanted a carnal relation with other men. This act is of the basest sort.

I thought that this was interesting, look with me in, Genesis 18:20, & 21- *And the LORD said, Because the cry of Sodom and Gomorrah is great, and because their sin is very grievous; I will go down now, and see whether they have done altogether according to the cry of it, which is come unto me; and if not, I will know.*

There are a couple of things I see in these verses. First, the cry of Sodom. I've often wondered what these cries were? Second, who was the one crying?

We see in 2 Peter 2:7-*And delivered just Lot, vexed with the filthy conversation of the wicked: (For that righteous man dwelling among them, in seeing and hearing, vexed his righteous soul from day to day with their unlawful deeds;)* The word just means *righteous.* The word vexed means *afflicted, or troubled.*

I wonder if the cry of Sodom, were the cries of Lot. I wonder if Lot was in prayer for the people of Sodom. Lot knowing their wickedness, may have been lifting them to God in hopes of them repenting from their wicked ways. Or, could the cries have come from someone else?

In Ezekiel 16:49-50-*Behold, this was the iniquity of thy sister Sodom, pride, fullness of bread, and abundance of idleness was in her and in her daughters, neither did she strengthen the hand of the poor and needy. And they were haughty, and committed abomination before me: therefore I took them away as I saw good.*

It could very well have been the cries of the poor and needy. God, sees how even the wicked treat those who are without. If God judged the wicked for this crime against the poor and needy, what do you think He will do to us that close our hearts to our brethren that are in need, and without. You and I know better....

Then we have the second definition of <u>fornication</u>; *adultery.* In Jeremiah 23:14-*I have seen also in the prophets of Jerusalem an horrible thing: they commit adultery, and walk in lies: they strengthen also the hands of evildoers, that none doth return from his wickedness: they are all of them unto me as Sodom, and the inhabitants thereof as Gomorrah.* God refers to the prophets of Jerusalem as adulterers *(as Sodom, and the inhabitants thereof as Gomorrah.)*

These two cities were guilty of this wicked lifestyle. God gave them Lot for a witness, but did they listen to him? No. They continued in their adulterous sin, until God had enough. God gives all of us a space to repent. What we decide in that time decides our fate.

The third definition of <u>fornication</u> is *incest.* We find this in the book of Genesis chapter 19: 30-38-*And Lot went up out of Zoar, and dwelt in the mountain, and his two daughters with him; for he feared to dwell in Zoar: and he dwelt in a cave, he and his two daughters. And the firstborn said unto the younger, Our father is old, and there is not a man in the earth to come in unto us after the manner of all the earth: Come, let us make our father drink wine, and we will lie with him, that we may preserve seed of our father. And they made their father drink wine that night: and the firstborn went in, and lay with her father; and he perceived not when she lay down, nor when she arose. And it came to pass on the morrow, that the firstborn said unto the younger, Behold, I lay yesternight with my father: let us make him drink wine this night also; and go thou in, and lie with him, that we may preserve seed of our father. And they made their father drink wine that night also: and the younger arose, and lay with him; and he perceived not when she lay down, nor when she arose. Thus were both the daughters of Lot with child by their father. And the firstborn bare a son, and called his name Moab: the same is the father of the Moabites unto this day. And the younger, she also bare a son, and called his name Benammi: the same is the father of the children of Ammon unto this day.*

Because these girls were raised in a wicked environment and probably had wicked friends, I don't know how they were still virgins, to begin with, but they were. The immoral philosophy of Sodom and Gomorrah had so corrupted the thinking of them both that they unhesitatingly contrived to be impregnated by their own father.

Let me interject this; It's important to know who our children hang out with, where they spend their time and how they spend their time. Our job as a parent isn't hanging out in our man cave, men. Nor is it going to the spa with the girlfriends while neglecting your children, ladies.

These girls evidently had no moral influence in their life. And because of this, they thought nothing of committing incest with their father, after they got him drunk.

The fourth definition of <u>Fornication</u>; *Idolatry*. Look at Deuteronomy 29:23-27-**And that the whole land thereof is brimstone, and salt, and burning, that it is not sown, nor beareth, nor any grass groweth therein, like the overthrow of Sodom, and Gomorrah, Admah, and Zeboim, which the Lord overthrew in his anger, and in his wrath: Even all nations shall say, wherefore hath the Lord done thus unto this land? what meaneth the heat of this great anger? Then men shall say, because they have forsaken the covenant of the Lord God of their fathers, which he made with them when he brought them forth out of the land of Egypt: For they went and served other gods, and worshipped them, gods whom they knew not, and whom he had not given unto them: And the anger of the Lord was kindled against this land, to bring upon it all the curses that are written in this book.**

Yes, I believe that these two cities were guilty of fornication in every aspect. God hates fornication of any kind. Listen to this verse; Genesis 13:13-**But the men of Sodom were wicked and sinners before the Lord exceedingly.**

<u>Wicked</u> means *Evil in principle and practice*. <u>Exceedingly</u> means *in a degree beyond what is usual*. In a nutshell, this was Sodom and Gomorrah. I'm starting to fear for America. How about you? Where does America fit into this definition? Where are we at today in America? I fear that we've gone too far.

But as Abraham would ask, "what if there were fifty righteous?" Let me just say this, I don't know personally of fifty righteous, I couldn't name you that many people that I would say are righteous.

God told Solomon in a dream: 2 Chronicles 7:14-*If my people, which are called by my name, shall humble themselves, and pray, and seek my face, and turn from their wicked ways; then will I hear from heaven, and will forgive their sin, and will heal their land.*

Where are the righteous today? Where are they? We should be on our knees begging God to take America back, it used to be a nation with morals but no more. We once ruled this nation under God, with Liberty, but no more! Where are the voices of Christians being heard at today?

We've lost our country, so that we could live comfortably, so we could drive nice cars, so we could go on vacations, so we could have a fat pocketbook. We've prostituted ourselves to Satan for wealth, fame, luxuries! Wake up America! Wake up Christians! Wake up!

Enough ranting, let's look on. What was the fate of these two cities? Look at Genesis 19:23-28- *The sun was risen upon the earth when Lot entered into Zoar. Then the Lord rained upon Sodom and upon Gomorrah brimstone and fire from the Lord out of heaven; And he overthrew those cities, and all the plain, and all the inhabitants of the cities, and that which grew upon the ground.*

But his wife looked back from behind him, and she became a pillar of salt. And Abraham gat up early in the morning to the place where he stood before the Lord: And he looked toward Sodom and Gomorrah, and toward all the land of the plain, and beheld, and, lo, the smoke of the country went up as the smoke of a furnace. God will not allow any nation to continue in sin…. He won't. We will reap what we've sown.

Time after time, and verse after verse God shows us, and brings before our eyes in Scripture, the effects of His anger, not to brag but to warn us. Warn us that His hate for sin, brings about judgment. God reminds us though out Scripture that these cities are our examples of his wrath.

Going after strange flesh- We know that they were fornicators, but this term 'strange flesh' means homosexuality- let me show you; Genesis 19:5- *…bring them out unto us, that we may know them.* This doesn't mean that they wanted to be friends. The word <u>know</u> means *in an intimate way; sexually.*

Romans 1:26 & 27-*For this cause God gave them up unto vile affections: for even their women did change the natural use into that which is against nature: And likewise also the men, leaving the natural use of the woman, burned in their lust one toward another, men with men working that which is unseemly, and receiving in themselves that recompense of their error which was meet.*

This strange flesh- is vile, perverted, sickening to God. God abhors this lifestyle. the more a person condones it the further away they'll get from God's grace. We stand as a Christian by being a light, that shines in our community, that says "I'm a Christian, I have principles that I'm loyal to!! We are not to be loyal to parties, people, conventions, or places, over our loyalty to God.

Are set forth for an example- The reason why these cities keep appearing in Scripture is because, they are set forth for an example. To who? To us. We forget too often where sin leads us. We forget that God has a day of Judgment set, we don't want to be guilty of this immorality on that day.

Suffering the vengeance of eternal fire- Where did the inhabitants of these cities go? Hell! God loves us, so He warns us, constantly. God says to us through Scripture, "Don't do it!" He cries out. "Repent! Get right!" He wishes no one to go to hell, but sadly most will not listen.

Jude was warning the readers of this epistle, and through it God is now warning us. As always, we need to learn from the mistakes that we see in the illustrations of the Bible, and don't make the same ones.

Jude 8-Likewise also these filthy dreamers defile the flesh, despise dominion, and speak evil of dignities.

Likewise also these filthy dreamers- Def. of <u>Filthy</u> *Polluted; defiled by sinful practices.* Def. of <u>Dreamers</u> *A man lost in wild imagination.*

Jude was referring to those he was speaking about in verse 4. These apostates were perverts, with pornographic minds, constantly perverting every thought. They were incapable of pure thoughts because they had rejected the living God. Today, you and I need to constantly guard against corrupt imaginations. Guard your thoughts. This is one area that all of us need to constantly work at.

Paul told us in Ephesians 6:17-***And take the helmet of salvation....*** This helmet that Paul spoke of is an important piece of Christian armor. Without it, the Christian is defenseless from Satan's brutal attacks against his mind.

Think with me for a minute in your own life; you are most susceptible to sin when you're not thinking about eternal things, such as God, salvation, or heaven. These things hold a holy presence in our minds. The reason that most of us as Christians have perverted minds and can't ever say no to sin or we never think to read and study our Bibles is because we don't ever pick up our helmet of salvation and strap it on. We've misplaced it, and frankly most Christians don't care to look for it.

Most Christians today don't have assurance of their salvation, and this is because they are NOT close to God. They don't have a true relationship with the Father, so the Holy Spirit is constantly being grieved.

If you personally do not have assurance of your salvation, then think with me for a moment; When was the last time you picked up your Bible to read it? When was the last time that you took time out of your day to pray? When was the last time that you could resist sin? It's possible that you may have misplaced your helmet of salvation. Not your salvation, but your helmet.

How often are you thinking on perverted things? How often men, do you see a woman out somewhere that is attractive and the first thing you do is to try to mentally undress her? If you do, then you are a pervert. The reason is that you have no relationship with the Father.

When was the last time you've memorized a verse of Scripture? When was the last time you've seen your prayers answered? What kind of relationship do you have with God? Think about this for a minute, I'm not trying to get on you, I want to help you. Sometimes we need to be scolded.

Defile the flesh- <u>Defile</u> *to taint, in a moral sense; to corrupt; render impure with sin.* We know what Paul told us in 1Corinthians 3:16,17-*Know ye not that ye are the temple of God, and that the Spirit of God dwelleth in you? If any man defile the temple of God, him shall God destroy; for the temple of God is holy, which temple ye are.* When was the last time that we've sat down and meditated upon this verse? It's convicting. Jude said; *likewise these filthy dreamers defile the flesh....*

He didn't say their flesh, only **the flesh**. These perverts don't care whose flesh they defile, they are only concerned about defiling the flesh. Yours, theirs, your children. I have news for you, God doesn't put up with this from His children.

Look at this verse, 1 Corinthians 3:17-*If any man defile the temple of God, him shall God destroy....* How does our body become defiled? with sin. <u>Defile</u> means *corrupt or to destroy.* This is the after effect of sin in our life.

Look at 1 Timothy 1:10-*For whoremongeres, for them that defile themselves with mankind, for men stealers, for liars, for perjured persons, and if there be any other thing that is contrary to sound doctrine;* Paul was telling Timothy, look, the law was made for these people. What does this term mean? *"Them that defile themselves with mankind"* This is speaking specifically of the sin of Sodomy. That is to defile yourself with mankind, to corrupt, to render impure with sin.

This is total wickedness. No one in their right mind would approve of these acts. That's why those who do so aren't in their right mind. Their flesh is in control.

Look at 2 Peter 2:10-*But chiefly them that walk after the flesh in the lust of uncleanness, and despise government. Presumptuous are they, self willed, they are not afraid to speak evil of dignities.*

Their lives are controlled by their flesh, lusting after everything that is desirable to the flesh. I've heard arguments about whether a Christian could or couldn't commit such acts. I won't debate anyone over it, but my opinion is this, I believe that a Christian can get so low in life, get so worldly, so backsliden, that they could commit just as an abomination of sins as anyone that is lost. Examples in Scripture would be David, Solomon, Lot. I could go on. There is no limit to how far into sin anyone can go. The question is how far down in sin are you today?

Yes! You can commit the most heinous crimes and you can act just like the lost world out there. Why? Because you have a sin nature, and if you allow it to take root in your heart, to take control, it will rip it to pieces.

Despise dominion- Despise- *to abhor; hate extremely, or with contempt.* Dominion-*Sovereign or supreme authority; an order of angels; persons governed.*

The Bible gives us plenty of illustrations of this; Genesis 3:5- *For God doth know that in the day ye eat thereof, then your eyes shall be opened, and ye shall be as god's, knowing good and evil.* Here Satan, the ultimate despiser of dominion, especially God's dominion, deceives Eve and persuades Adam into taking the fruit from the tree of the knowledge of good and evil and to eat of it.

Psalms 12:3,4-*The LORD shall cut off all flattering lips, and the tongue that speaks proud things: Who have said with our tongue will we prevail; our lips are our own: who is lord over us?* Those that despise dominion God will judge. It's not our fight. When one speaks against God, then God will deal with them.

And speak evil of dignities- Dignities *an elevated office, civil or ecclesiastical, giving a high rank in society; advancement; preferment, or the rank attached to it.* Looking at Numbers 16:3-*And they gathered themselves together against Moses and against Aaron, and said unto them, ye take too much upon you, seeing all the congregation are holy, every one of them, and the LORD is among them: wherefore then lift ye up yourselves above the congregation of the LORD?*

In this verse, three men revolted against Moses and God. They felt it was their duty to stand against them, but, we know that in the end that God showed the congregation who He put in charge.

Then over in Exodus 22:28-*Thou shalt not revile the gods, nor curse the ruler of the people.* The word gods in this verse, means *ruler or judge, someone who is placed in authority.* That means, even our president, our senate, our house of reps, our judges on the Supreme Court. As much as I would love to speak evil of these people, my God tells me that we had better not. It's not our place to do so.

With that in mind, how much have you and I already disobeyed God in this verse? I know that I'm guilty of it. No I don't like what America has turned into, but God tells me that I had better keep my mouth shut if all I should say about the leadership in America is evil.

Today, I fear God. I'd rather tell him my concerns than to tell others. God says that it is evil of us to speak bad of those over us. Look at what I Peter 2:17 says- *Honor all men. Love the brotherhood. Fear God. Honor the king.*

Honor means *to treat with due civility and respect in the ordinary intercourse of life.* We are to obey God, lest we become pious as the Israelites were in that they saw the hand of God move with power on the Egyptians while God was preserving their own lives. They bickered and complained about Moses and God, until God had enough and judged them then and there. Yes, we are loved by God but that does not buy us the freedom to act and speak as we please. We are Christians and should act as such.

Unless we forget that our God is a consuming fire, lest we forget that God said in Colossians 1:16-*For by him were all things created, that are in heaven, and that are in earth, visible and invisible, whether they be thrones, or dominions, or principalities, or powers: all things were created by him, and for him:*

It's God's business who is in the White House and at the twinkling of an eye, He could change it as His sees fit. We often forget that God knows what He is doing, don't we? Often, we are at the edge of our seats wondering how this is going to play out, never realizing that God sees the end just as well as He saw the beginning, and also sees now.

Remember that Jude was speaking of those in verse four, those certain men, but he was worried that these men had snuck into the church to apostatize it. Today, are you guilty of any of the sins that were discussed in this chapter? You, not your spouse, or friend or neighbor, but are you? Take time to pray and ask God to clean you of any unrighteousness that you may hold inside.

Jude 9-Yet Michael the archangel, when contending with the devil he disputed about the body of Moses, durst not bring against him a railing accusation, but said, The Lord rebuke thee.

Yet Michael the archangel- With this part of the verse we find ourselves asking two questions; Who is this Michael and what is an archangel? An <u>Archangel</u> is *an Angel of the highest order;* From what I have gathered in the Bible, Michael is the chief angel under the command of God. He assumed this position once Satan rebelled against God. When the rebellion took place, God threw Satan out of heaven, along with his followers.

He is spoken of in several passages of Scripture; Daniel 10:13-*But the prince of the kingdom of Persia withstood me one and twenty days: but, Lo, Michael, one of the chief princes, came to help me....* In this passage, Daniel had prayed to God and God answered his prayer sending an angel to him, but the angel was hindered for 21 days by Satan, until he received help from Michael the archangel.

This tells me that Michael has some pull, he has some power and authority, not of his own, but given to him by God. Then in verse 21 of the same chapter of Daniel we read; *But I will shew thee that which is noted in the Scripture of truth: and there is none that holdeth with me in these things, but Michael your prince.*

It has been said that Michael is a guardian angel for the Jewish people; that he has special charge of their affairs; that his interposition might be depended on the time of trouble or danger, and that, under him, their interests would be safe. -BARNES.

We see his name again in chapter 12:1-*And at that time shall Michael stand up, the great prince which standeth for the children of thy people....* See Michael is looked at as a great protector of Israel, and is called a prince.

Then we see his name mentioned in Revelation 12:7-*And there was war in heaven: Michael and his angels fought against the dragon; and the dragon fought and his angels,.* After reading this verse, I can't see angels looking feminine. I see them as you would picture a cowboy back in the old wild west. Rough looking, scars, unshaven, tobacco juice dripping off their chin.

This verse also tells me that since Michael is the only one mentioned by name, afterward it says (and his angels), that he is the head or chief of the angels. But, only under the authority of God.

35

Michael has been called by several names; Daniel 10:13- *one of the chief princes;* Daniel 12:1- *the great prince.*

The fascinating thing about Michael is what's written in I Thessalonians 4:16-*For the Lord himself shall descend from heaven with a shout, with the voice of the archangel, and with the trump of God: and the dead in Christ shall rise first:* This verse is referring to the coming of the Lord or what we commonly refer to as the rapture. This verse tells us four different things that will happen at once; first, the Lord will descend from heaven. Second, the Lord will give a shout and this will awake the dead and summon the saints to glory. Third, the voice of the archangel,which is Michael, I believe he is sounding the beginning of the Tribulation, and his voice will assemble the angelic hosts and marshal them in for their leading role of the end-time events. Forth, the trump of God sounding –this will alert Israel and hasten the regathering of the Jews to the Promise Land. This is pictured in the Old Testament of God sounding the trumpet and the Israelites gathering together.

Not to get side tracked but I wanted to point out that Michael has an important job to do concerning the last days. I'm sure that we don't know all the details of what Michael's duties are, but I know that he stays busy about God's work.

I wanted to share with you a few facts that I've learned about angels while studying this.

1. Angels do not marry- Matthew 22:30
2. Angels are immortal- Luke 20:35-36
3. Angels are invisible- Col. 1:16. Though they can be visible…
4. Angels are created sprits and are appointed to minister and serve- Hebrews 1:7, 14
5. Angels are God's messengers and his servants- Ps. 104:4; Hebrews 1:7

Here is one I thought to be very interesting concerning the difference between mankind and angels; Adam fell into sin, but the second Adam (Jesus) has come to redeem him, Rom 5:12, 19; 1 Cor. 15:45. Angels fell into sin but are not redeemed by Jesus Christ. (Hebrews 2:16.)

Let's move on with this verse.

When contending with the devil he disputed about the body of Moses- Contending means *striving; struggling to oppose; debating or quarreling.* The Devil- goes by many names;

1. Serpent-first used in Genesis when the devil took possession of the snake to deceive Eve.

2. Satan-first used in Chronicles when the devil tempted David to number the people.

3. Lucifer- a proper name used only once, given by Isaiah, while describing his fall from heaven.

I thought it an interesting fact to note that the name "devil" is only used in the New Testament. It was used 57 times, but 39 of those times in the gospels alone.

Disputed means *to separate oneself in a hostile spirit, to oppose, strive with.* Now this is a very interesting part of the verse. Nowhere else in Scripture does it speak of Satan and Michael disputing over the body of Moses.

Now I said earlier that Jude does reference some Apocryphal books not that he sees those books as being inspired but, he is gleaning bits of history from them. Of course, we know that God inspired Jude to do so.

***Note: the first century church debated whether to include Jude in the Canon because of this verse and a few others that mention events that are only spoken of in the Apocryphal books. Nevertheless, God's hand was involved and He, as always, is in control of the situation.

To better understand this verse, we need to go back to Deuteronomy 34:5,6-*So Moses the servant of the LORD died there in the land of Moab, according to the word of the LORD. And he buried him in a valley in the land of Moab, over against Bethpeor; but no man knoweth of his sepulcher unto this day.* So, we see that God had Moses buried secretly so that no man would know where he was buried. God does not give reason for this only that it was done.

May I insert, nor does God need to give a reason…Did you hear me? God does not have to answer to us. He is in control not us.

Durst not bring against him a railing accusation, but said the Lord rebuke thee- Jude recorded that for some reason Satan wanted the body of Moses, no known reason why but speculation is that he wanted to make an idol of it so the Israelites would worship it, just as they did the brazen serpent that Moses had made. For more on the brazen serpent you can look up these verses; Numbers 21:5-9 and 2 kings 18:4.

This part of the verse can easily become deep. For some scholars believe that **the body of Moses** was attributed to the nation of Israel whereas the "body of Christ" represents the church. It could be that Satan was asking God to reattribute punishment to the nation for their utterly adulterous lifestyle. I.E- Idolatry, fornication, etc. I don't agree with this, but thought it worth repeating anyway.

This part of the verse coincides with part of verse 8; *"and speak evil of dignities"* We see that Peter also spoke of this in 2 Peter 2:11-*Whereas angels, which are greater in power and might, bring not railing accusation against them before the Lord.*

It also reminds me of Zechariah 3:2-*And the Lord said unto Satan, the LORD rebuke thee, O Satan; even the Lord that hath chosen Jerusalem rebuke thee: is not this the brand plucked out of the fire?*

As I said, Michael knows the position that Satan once held in heaven, (the top position within the Angels.) He knew where he stood. So instead of Michael railing against Satan, he gave the fight to God.

This reminds me how many dog fights we get ourselves into when we should have just given it unto the Lord. This is exactly how God wants us to live our lives.

Look at what Paul said in Romans 12:19-*Dearly beloved, avenge not yourselves, but rather give place unto wrath: for it is written, vengeance is mine; I will repay, saith the Lord.*

All too often we want to take part of a fight that isn't ours. Vengeance belongs to God and so do many of our fights. Also, I want to point out that if Michael didn't bring accusation to Satan, how in this world do we think that we can do so, lest we forget that we were made a little lower than the angels.

Let's take a minute to review this verse. First, sometimes the Bible isn't clear on where the author received their information from concerning past events, such as Genesis which tells us a lot concerning creation. This is where faith comes in.

God has made known to us these events through His word, and by faith we receive the Bible as being inspired writing. There are many things that we must do this with, not just with information in the Bible.

You and I have problems in this life and by faith we must learn to trust God and obey His word. It isn't always easy, but God tells us to trust Him, and I've experienced that the more I trust Him the more I see His hand working in my life. This helps me to live by faith, and it builds my faith also.

Today, I have no problems with believing anything that the Bible says about any topic. I believe every word of it! I know it's God's word and I don't have to question it. How about you? Do you believe that the Bible is God's word, and that it is infallible? Do you have any doubts that He is telling you the truth about any matter?

Jude did indeed write about some topics that are not given or explained in any other book of the Bible. However, this shouldn't hinder us from trusting that Jude is indeed part of God's word.

You and I are going to get into scuffles with Satan and his fallen angels, that is if you are living for God. We are given the example in this verse that it's not our fight, give it to God. Allow Him to take care of the situation. He can handle it.

Jude 10-**But these speak evil of those things which they know not: but what they know naturally, as brute beasts, in those things they corrupt themselves.**

But these speak evil of those things which they know not- In studying this passage, I found that this entire verse coincides closely with 2 Peter 2:12-*But these, as natural brute beasts made to be taken and destroyed, speak evil of the things that they understand not; and shall utterly perish in their own corruption.* The wording of these two passages are remarkable in their similarities.

If you know anything about chapter two of 2 Peter, you will know that he was warning against false prophets and false teachers. Clearly the same message that Jude is warning his readers of. Nothing has changed. It is still an issue now as it was back in their day. It still needs to be taught to the church today.

I know that I sound like a broken record but the reason why so many churches have lowered their convictions and their standards is because they have allowed these *'certain men to creep in unawares.'*

A degree doesn't mean a hill of beans for a preacher if he doesn't believe in the Bible as being the Word of God. Recommendations from the finest of colleges doesn't mean a hill of beans for a preacher if he doesn't believe in the virgin birth of our Lord. Good looks and a suave personality doesn't mean a hill of beans for a preacher if he thinks that the creation story is just a fabrication of someone's imagination. Give me a man of God that stands on God's Word. I'll take that over a diploma, recommendations and good looks.

Give me a man of God that preaches the Bible instead of his opinion. Make sure you have a man of God with a backbone that will stand on God's word instead of trying to please the congregation or the Deacon board. If you give heresy an inch it will destroy the entire church.

There are churches across this land that licentious persons on their staff. How did this happen? It did not happen overnight. Heresy crept in little by little and changed the way their congregations viewed sin.

Why can't we call sin by its name, sin? It must be called something else, like an addiction, a problem or weakness. These things are sin. Nothing short of it either.

This is exactly how America's churches have become like that too. It wasn't overnight, but little by little, some apostate preacher, some apostate deacon, some apostate church member persuaded the congregation to be more approving, more tolerant. We are not to be tolerant of sin; people yes, sin no! As Barney Fife would say you must "nip it in the bud." You can't allow sin to take root in your church.

Let's go on with our study. These *'certain men,'* these *'filthy dreamers'* they speak of the things of God as if they know God, to which they are completely ignorant of.

In 1 Corinthians 2:14-*But the natural man receiveth not the things of the Spirit of God: for they are foolishness unto him: neither can he know them, because they are spiritually discerned.* These false teachers, these carnal men are spoken of also in Colossians 2:18-*Let no man beguile you of your reward in a voluntary humility and worshipping of Angels, intruding into those things which he hath not seen, vainly puffed by his fleshly mind.*

We have a perfect illustration of this in Acts 19:24-41-*For a certain man named Demetrius, a silversmith, which made silver shrines for Diana, brought no small gain unto the craftsmen; Whom he called together with the workmen of like occupation, and said, Sirs, ye know that by this craft we have our wealth. Moreover ye see and hear, that not alone at Ephesus, but almost throughout all Asia, this Paul hath persuaded and turned away much people, saying that they be no gods, which are made with hands: So that not only this our craft is in danger to be set at nought; but also that the temple of the great goddess Diana should be despised, and her magnificence should be destroyed, whom all Asia and the world worshippeth. And when they heard these sayings, they were full of wrath, and cried out, saying, Great is Diana of the Ephesians. And the whole city was filled with confusion: and having caught Gaius and Aristarchus, men of Macedonia, Paul's companions in travel, they rushed with one accord into the theatre. And when Paul would have entered in unto the people, the disciples suffered him not. And certain of the chief of Asia, which were his friends, sent unto him, desiring him that he would not adventure himself into the theatre. Some therefore cried one thing, and some another: for the assembly was confused; and the more part knew not wherefore they were come together. And they drew Alexander out of the multitude, the Jews putting him forward. And Alexander beckoned with the hand, and would have made his defence unto the people. But when they knew that he was a Jew, all with one voice about the space of two hours cried out, Great is Diana*

41

of the Ephesians. And when the townclerk had appeased the people, he said, ye men of Ephesus, what man is there that knoweth not how that the city of the Ephesians is a worshipper of the great goddess Diana, and of the image which fell down from Jupiter? Seeing then that these things cannot be spoken against, ye ought to be quiet, and to do nothing rashly. For ye have brought hither these men, which are neither robbers of churches, nor yet blasphemers of your goddess. Wherefore if Demetrius, and the craftsmen which are with him, have a matter against any man, the law is open, and there are deputies: let them implead one another. But if ye enquire any thing concerning other matters, it shall be determined in a lawful assembly. For we are in danger to be called in question for this day's uproar, there being no cause whereby we may give an account of this concourse. And when he had thus spoken, he dismissed the assembly.

Now let's review these verses. I think that this will help us understand better what Jude was speaking of in verse ten of his epistle.

Starting in verse 24-***For a certain man named Demetrius, a silversmith....*** The story starts with a silversmith named Demetrius; he was responsible for this man-made idol of the Greek goddess Artemis, which we know as Diana. He calls a meeting with other smiths, concerned about the welfare of their trade.

In verse 26, he states that they have seen and heard the results of Paul's labor. Not only was Paul winning converts in Ephesus but throughout all of Asia. Demetrius' concern was what Paul preached;***'they be no god's, which are made with hands.'*** I could see how that might affect Demetrius' finances.

In verse 27, he continues to show concern stating ***'our craft is in danger and the temple should be despised and her magnificence should be destroyed.'*** He worshipped this goddess himself, probably more so due to his financial gain than anything else.

In verse 28, by his speech he causes the men to become ***'full of wrath.'***

In verse 29, evidently, they set about the city, full of wrath, confusing the people of the city. The men grab two of Paul's companions, 'Gaius and Aristarchus' and they rushed them into the city's theater.

Paul saw what was happening. He wanted to enter the theater with his friends but was restrained by others who most likely feared the outcome.

In verse 32, mass confusion was set upon the crowd.

In verse 34 (this is unbelievable) for two hours the mob cried out '**Great is Diana of the Ephesians.**' The people in the theater recognized that Alexander (the one whom was trying to appease the crowd) was a Jew and this caused the two-hour outcry.

In verses 35 through 38, the town clerk stood up and quietened the crowd. He began his speech by beckoning the crowd to disperse for these reasons; first, '**all know that the Ephesians worship Diana and the image that fell from Jupiter.**' Second, the men that were brought forth, 'Gaius and Aristarchus,' weren't thieves nor blasphemes of their goddess. Third, if there is a legitimate issue, the law was open. Lastly, If the higher authority got wind of this uprising, then they would be in trouble! In verse 41, the town clerk dismissed the assembly.

Question- Who was this Man Demetrius? He was a pagan idol maker, He rejected the truth that Paul preached, and was willing to start a commotion to protect his wicked lifestyle. Did you see how this was a perfect illustration of verse 10 of Jude? Let's look it again; **But these speak evil of those things which they know not.**

But what they know naturally, as brute beasts, in those things they corrupt themselves- Look with me at Romans 1:21,22-*Because that, when they knew God, they glorified him not as God, neither were thankful; but became vain in their imaginations, and their foolish heart was darkened. Professing themselves to be wise, they became fools.*

To understand Romans, you must realize Paul's reason for writing Romans. It was to explain that salvation is offered through the gospel of Jesus Christ. For man to understand that he needs this salvation that our Lord offers, he must first realize that he is a sinner.

After a brief greeting, Paul, starting in 1:17, explained man's lost and most deprived condition. These verses show man in his fullest capacity without God. Notice that I said without God, not without the knowledge of God.

Romans chapter one verse 21 states '*when they knew God*' they knew who God was, though they did not want to regard him as God. They wanted nothing to do with Him, nor were they thankful, but their perverted minds were filled with empty or worthless (*vain*) imaginations.

These were the basest of men, vile, perverts of the highest rank. Because of this, their foolish heart was <u>darkened</u> meaning *made ignorant.*

That's why in verse 22 they professed to be wise, and quite possibly they were in the fields of science or math, but concerning the things of God, *'they became fools.'*

Demetrius was a silversmith, probably taught as a trade by his father. This is what he knew naturally, but in denying God as Paul preached, he became as a brute beast, and *'in those things they corrupt themselves.'*

Look with me in Philippians 3:18, 19- *(For many walk, of whom I have told you often, and now tell you even weeping, that they are the enemies of the cross of Christ: Whose end is destruction, whose God is their belly, and whose glory is in their shame, who mind earthly things.)* Do you think that Demetrius was an enemy of the cross? Yes.

Today you and I have the responsibility to guard our children, our grandchildren from these enemies of the 'cross of Christ'. That means making hard decisions and sometimes making unpopular ones too.

The number one thing in our lives should be God. So, it's important to make sure you are going to a church that expounds God's word. If you are a part of a body of believers that teaches God's word, then you are ahead of the game. There are too many churches today that lack solid biblical preaching and teaching.

If you are a parent, then don't forfeit your children's future of solid biblical learning because of finances or friends. It's not worth it. God can supply all of those needs that you deem important. What He wants from you and I is our faithfulness to the Word of God.

Today, have you given any thought to how you can protect your family from the Demetrius' of this world? What is it that you can do to provide them with the absolute best biblical teaching?

First, all good teachers (parents you are teacher too) must be good role models. Proverbs 23:23-*Buy the truth, and sell it not;* What I mean is don't sell out! Guard your church from apostates. Don't let them come in to teach, preach or hold offices. That will kill your church.

Lastly, center your life and family around God, His word and Prayer. Let us as Christians get back to being Christians.

Jude was telling his readers that these certain men, these filthy dreamers, creep into your churches and destroy it from the inside. He said to watch out for preachers that don't preach the Bible. Watch out for preachers who only have a music show and no preaching. Watch out for preachers that get behind the pulpit and tell an hour of life stories and never feed you God's

Word. Watch out for them. They are deceivers. Those that are always correcting God's word as if it needs it, don't give them your time.

Jude was warning them of these apostates. Today, he warns us so we will not have the same issues the early church was having.

Note to the Reader

Keep in mind that while we study the book of Jude that he was warning his dedicated readers to keep a watch over the church and over their own faith. Not to get duped or persuaded to follow hearsay.

In this next verse, verse 11, he gave three keen examples to show exactly how that, if someone is not careful he may fall into the same sins as others.

We need to remember that we are not our own, for we have been bought with a price as Paul stated in I Corinthians 6:19 & 20-*What? Know ye not that your body is the temple of the Holy Ghost which is in you, which ye have of God, and ye are not your own? For ye are bought with a price: therefore, glorify God in your body, and in your spirit, which are God's.*

Did you get that? Jude, pleaded with his readers and with us, not to get caught up in these acts of wickedness, why? For we're bought by the precious blood of Jesus Christ!

Our problem is that we haven't sold out to God yet. We want to hold on to our old lifestyle, thinking that it wasn't so bad. That's not how it works. God purchased us and we have no right to go back to that old lifestyle, that old way of thinking and acting.

God has too much invested in us for you and I to become vain in our thinking. We must always keep the cross before our minds, for when we lose sight of it, failure, destruction and misery is just over the hill.

So, let's go ahead and begin this new section of Jude.

Jude 11-**Woe unto them! For they have gone in the way of Cain, and ran greedily after the error of Balaam for reward, and perished in the gain saying of Korah.**

Woe unto them- First we need to look at this interjection; **Woe.** In studying I was led to Isaiah 3:9-*The shew of their countenance doth witness against them; and they declare their sin as Sodom, they hide it not. Woe unto their soul! For they have rewarded evil unto themselves.*

First, who was Jude speaking about? Look at a few verses with me in Jude. Start with 4-*for there are certain men crept in unawares.* Now look at 8-*these filthy dreamers.* Here is 10-*but these speak evil of these things.*

It's the same group of people throughout the epistle. He was speaking of these apostates. I've found that in discerning between genuine Christians and wolves, it's easy to spot the difference. You only need to pay close attention to the signs.

Isaiah said- *the shew of their countenance doth witness against them.* It's the same with the apostates, the love of God is nowhere shown upon them. They are full of wickedness. Only the ignorant will be fooled. But sadly, most church members are indeed ignorant. Isaiah said- *they declare their sin as Sodom, they hide it not.*

These are proud to say that same sex marriage is biblical, or that there is no difference between our lifestyle and that of the worlds. They don't hide the fact that they believe the Bible to be old and outdated. But I'm here to tell you that they are wrong.

Lastly Isaiah said- *for they have rewarded evil unto themselves.* Their destruction awaits them. All they have to look forward to is hell.

Next Jude gave three illustrations from the Old Testament. One of each of the following men: Cain, Balaam and Korah. With each illustration, we will see how apostasy attacks the salvation, the sovereignty, and the service of God.

For they have gone in the way of Cain- Who is this Cain? I know that we discussed this a little in the introduction, but let's dig in the Scriptures now to find out who Cain was, and why he was named by Jude as having his own way.

First, Cain was the very first baby ever born. His parents were Adam and Eve. We see this in Genesis 4:1.

Second, he had a younger brother named Abel, seen in Genesis 4:2. For some reason jealousy crept into Cain's heart concerning Abel and this caused Cain to sin. Third, we see that Cain was a tiller of the ground while his younger brother was a sheep herder. Now both jobs were very important in that day. Although, men and women were vegetarians during this time, sheep were still needed for clothing.

We see in verse 3-*And in the process of time it came to pass,* the wording of this verse leads me to believe that there was an appointed time in which the people were to bring to God an offering, may very well not have been a sacrifice but indeed an offering of some sort.

You know, I've heard and, I'm sure that you also have heard, many messages concerning this one verse. Some messages say that it was to be an offering of blood, others stated that it didn't matter about it being of blood so long as it was the best you have.

I remember a message that Dr. Hyles, who was once the pastor of First Baptist Church of Hammond, IN, preached on this concerning the offering. He stated that the issue was that Abel gave of his first fruits and Cain didn't, meaning that Abel tithed and Cain didn't.

Everyone has their opinions on this one, and I'm going to try and show you what I've studied out of the Bible concerning this issue so we can get to the heart of the matter, it being very important to why Jude stated what he did about him.

Ok, so we are at the point that Cain offered his fruit and veggies to the Lord. In verse 5-*But unto Cain and to his offering He had not respect.* Why was it that God in verse four, had respect to Abel's? What was the difference? Cain brought an offering unto the Lord, and it states that Abel brought of the firstlings of his flock and the fat thereof.

That term firstling meaning *it was the first of the litter, may even imply that it was the very best that he had.* Then the term the fat thereof meaning *the very best he had.* Now at this point the Bible says at the end of verse 5-*And Cain was very wroth, and his countenance fell.*

Why would this set Cain over the edge? Look at what John said about Cain. 1 John 3:12-*Not as Cain, who was of that wicked one, and slew his brother. And wherefore slew he him? Because his own works were evil, and his brother's righteous.*

John stated that Cain was of that wicked one and that his own works were evil. Therefore, his offering was not accepted. Cain was wroth because his offering was not accepted, because it was not presented to God in the proper way. It wasn't the best he had nor was it what God wanted.

Hosea 6:6-*For I desired mercy, and not sacrifice;* God had rather for Cain to showed Abel mercy than to have given Himself an offering. I want you to understand what I am about to say. Offerings have always been about the condition of the heart. Where do you stand with God when you give an offering? What I mean is your money, your time and your talents.

How's your heart when you give these things? Is it out of joy that you give financially? Is it out of love that you use your talents for God? How is your heart?

Look with me at Micah 6:6-8-*Wherewith shall I come before the LORD, and bow myself before the high God? Shall I come before him with burnt-offerings, with calves of a year old? Will the LORD be pleased with thousands of Rams, or with ten thousands of rivers of oil? Shall I give my firstborn for my transgression, the fruit of my body for the sin of my soul? He hath showed thee, O man, what is good; and what depth the LORD require of thee, but to do justly, and to love mercy, and to walk humbly with thy God?*

Does God desire burnt offerings? A multitude of offerings? Gifts? Human sacrifice? No! What does the Lord require of you? *But to do justly, and to love mercy, and to walk humbly with thy God.*

Then in Proverbs 21:27 we see *The sacrifice of the wicked is abomination: how much more, when he bringeth it with a wicked mind?*

These verses illustrate Cain in his wicked state. As Proverbs state with a wicked mind. Cain could have brought all the animals of the world and sacrificed them on the alter to God. But God never would have accepted it because as John stated; *because his own works were evil....* This was before the offering, during the offering and after the offering.

Cain was an unbelieving man, with no concern for the things of God. No concern for human life. Today, Cain is the perfect example of the unregenerate man.

Look at Genesis 4:5- *But unto Cain and to his offering he had not respect. And Cain was very wroth, and his countenance fell.* Cain was angry. At who? At God. Why? God didn't respect the offering that Cain provided. Why? It wasn't given by faith. Hebrews 11:6-*But without faith it is impossible to please him; for he that cometh to God must believe that he is, and that he is a rewarder of them that diligently seek him.*

Abel's offering was given to God by faith, Cain's wasn't. Cain, I believe ended up killing Abel because he was mad at God and there was no other way to hurt God but by murdering the one that He approved of.

Jude warned his readers not to go in the way of Cain. I believe that the way of Cain is more than just being a murderer. It's being an ungrateful human being. It's being careless of what God says we should and should not do.

We see discontent and disrespect when God was speaking to him about his brother. God asked him where Able was, his response was smart and unconcerned. Genesis 4:9-...*I know not: am I my brother's keeper?* But God's mercy and grace stepped in when you and I would probably have zapped him dead on the spot.

Instead of death, God punished Cain by taking his business from him. No longer would the earth yield her fruit to him. Also, he would wander the earth, a fugitive and a vagabond would he be. At no point, did Cain show a repentant heart, before or after his punishment. Only, we see his selfish mind when he responded to God's punishment; Genesis 4:13-... *My punishment is greater than I can bear.*

How's that for a man that was confronted about the murder of his brother. The saddest part of the entire story is verse sixteen; *And Cain went out from the presence of the Lord....*

Cain went on to build a great city and to have an enormous family. But the sad fact of the matter is that the Bible states that Cain left God's presence but it never says anything about him ever returning to Him. Cain, the first ever born in all the world, rejected God and caused grief to his family.

Today let's look at ourselves. Where are we at in this Christian walk? Jude's epistle is speaking to us even today. He begs us not to go *in the way of Cain.*

And ran greedily after the error of Balaam for reward- That little phrase, <u>ran greedily</u> means: *to follow with a keen appetite for material possession, to consume it upon yourself.* <u>Error</u>-*in Scripture and theology, is sin; iniquity; transgression.*

So, Jude was saying to his readers that these wicked individuals, those spoken of in verses 4 & 8, had a fleshly desire for sin, iniquity, and transgression. Just like that of Balaam. Their desires were for personal satisfaction, to consume it upon themselves.

My question today is what was the 'Error of Balaam?' Who was this Balaam and what sin did he commit that we need to be reminded of from Jude? Also, what did Balaam do that was so wrong, that you and I need to observe not to fall into that same iniquity?

We will get our story from the Old Testament book of Numbers chapter 22. In this chapter and the next two following it, Balaam is mentioned fifty times. Here we find that Balaam was a false prophet, and he was the son of Beor. The name <u>Beor</u> means *'to burn up'* while <u>Balaam's</u> name means *'destroyer or glutton.'*

Let's go ahead and look at Numbers 22. 1-6. *And the children of Israel set forward, and pitched in the plains of Moab on this side Jordan by Jericho. And Balak the son of Zippor saw all that Israel had done to the Amorites. And Moab was sore afraid of the people, because they were many: and Moab was distressed because of the children of Israel. And Moab said unto the elders of Midian, Now shall this company lick up all that are round about us, as the ox licketh up the grass of the field. And Balak the son of Zippor was king of the Moabites at that time. He sent messengers therefore unto Balaam the son of Beor to Pethor, which is by the river of the land of the children of his people, to call him, saying, Behold, there is a people come out from Egypt: behold, they cover the face of the earth, and they abide over against me: Come now therefore, I pray thee, curse me this people; for they are too mighty for me: peradventure I shall prevail, that we may smite them, and that I may drive them out of the land: for I wot that he whom thou blessest is blessed, and he whom thou cursest is cursed.*

Ok, we see in these verses that the children of Israel have encamped in the plain of Moab. Balak was then king of Moab. His fear was expressed in verses 2 & 3, that he saw all that Israel had done to the Amorites.

Now pay attention to verse 3-*now shall this company lick up all that are round about us, as the ox licketh up the grass of the field.* What Balak was saying is that he was only concerned that the Israelites would consume the natural resources, not that they would destroy his people, or Balak knew that they were near kin to the Israelites, being the offspring of Lot's incest with his firstborn daughter. We see this in Genesis 19:37-*and the firstborn bare a son, and called his name Moab: the same is the father of the Moabites unto this day.*

Then in verse 5 Balak sent messengers to a city called Pethor, by the river Euphrates. This city was just under 400 miles away from Moab. This was where the false prophet Balaam lived.

You know, in just reading this you wouldn't think that there's four hundred miles' distance from the one city to the other. The thing about reading the Bible and not ever studying it, is that you never get to see the time lapse between the verses. Most likely it took the men a month to get to Pethor.

We also see in verse five that Balak didn't want to be truthful enough to give Balaam the name of the people he needed cursed. This was held back as Balak knew that all the land far and wide had heard of the Israelites and the power of God among them. Note, "their God."

But we do see how Balak wanted the messengers to flatter Balaam, *"for I wot that he whom thou blessest is blessed, and he whom thou cursest is cursed."*

Here is Numbers 22:7-14-*And the elders of Moab and the elders of Midian departed with the rewards of divination in their hand; and they came unto Balaam, and spake unto him the words of Balak. And he said unto them, Lodge here this night, and I will bring you word again, as the Lord shall speak unto me: and the princes of Moab abode with Balaam. And God came unto Balaam, and said, What men are these with thee? And Balaam said unto God, Balak the son of Zippor, king of Moab, hath sent unto me, saying, Behold, there is a people come out of Egypt, which covereth the face of the earth: come now, curse me them; peradventure I shall be able to overcome them, and drive them out. And God said unto Balaam, Thou shalt not go with them; thou shalt not curse the people: for they are blessed. And Balaam rose up in the morning, and said unto the princes of Balak, Get you into your land: for the Lord refuseth to give me leave to go with you. And the princes of Moab rose up, and they went unto Balak, and said, Balaam refuseth to come with us.*

The messengers finally reached Balaam, and gave the request of the king to him. Balaam invited them to stay overnight for his answer. Somehow Balaam was going to ask the spirits or do some sort of demonstration with calling for an answer.

We see that the Lord spoke to him that night most likely in a dream as God did at other times to pagan men. Examples of this are Laban in *Genesis 31:24-And God came to Laban the Syrian in a dream by night, and said unto him....* And then Abimelech in *Genesis 20:3-But God came to Abimelech in a dream by night, and said to him....*

52

So, we see that it's not unusual for God to speak to heathen persons. Most likely Balaam asked who it was that was speaking to him. But we see in verse 8 that Balaam knew who the God of Israel was, for he called him by name. LORD meaning *YAHWEH,* which is the proper name of the God of Israel.

Though Balak made sure the messengers were not to be too specific on who he needed cursed, the Israelites were so well known that Balaam knew the name of their God. But as we see during these several chapters that he only knew His name, not God personally.

Next, I want us to look at the conversation that Balaam had with God. Not his god but the God of Israel. In verse 9-**And God came unto Balaam, and said, What men are these with thee?** You and I know that was a rhetorical question. But evidently, Balaam didn't. Look at his answer. Verse 10, 11-**And Balaam said unto God, Balak the son of Zippor, king of Moab, hath sent unto me, saying, Behold, there is a people come out of Egypt, which covereth the face of the earth: come now, curse me them; peradventure I shall be able to overcome them, and drive them out.**

I have a problem with Balaam's answer. He didn't give God the entire story. God, as a parent would a child, asked a rhetorical question, knowing the answer to it, with hope that the child would confess the entire story.

Balaam, the unregenerate prophet he was, held back the fact that their concern was financial and that they wanted to annihilate them.

The first thing we can learn from this story is, you and I as children of God need to remember that when we are being questioned whether it's by God, our boss, spouse or parents, that we are to be honest. Doing this does not allow for any doubt to creep in between you and the relationship of the other.

The problem with most Christians is that we are too worldly to realize that a white lie is still as sinful as any other lie. We've come to this dumb conclusion that we should lie rather than hurt someone's feelings, or that our spouse doesn't need to know everything we do.

If you want a stressful relationship with your spouse, then go ahead and lie, cheat, rob your character away from their minds. Honesty is always the best policy when it comes to spousal relationships.

Next, we see what God told Balaam, look at verse 12-**Thou shalt not go with them; thou shalt not curse the people: for they are blessed.** Pretty cut and dry, isn't it? I don't think that God was giving Balaam a suggestion on what He thought should be done.

So, Balaam went and gave word to the messengers that he couldn't go. The messengers went back to Balak, and told him all that happened. Balak then sent more messengers, the Bible says these messengers were *'more and more honorable then they.'*

Now we come to verses 16-21-*And they came to Balaam, and said to him, Thus saith Balak the son of Zippor, Let nothing, I pray thee, hinder thee from coming unto me: For I will promote thee unto very great honour, and I will do whatsoever thou sayest unto me: come therefore, I pray thee, curse me this people. And Balaam answered and said unto the servants of Balak, If Balak would give me his house full of silver and gold, I cannot go beyond the word of the Lord my God, to do less or more. Now therefore, I pray you, tarry ye also here this night, that I may know what the Lord will say unto me more. And God came unto Balaam at night, and said unto him, If the men come to call thee, rise up, and go with them; but yet the word which I shall say unto thee, that shalt thou do. And Balaam rose up in the morning, and saddled his ass, and went with the princes of Moab.*

They reached Balaam and begged him, and tried to bribe him to come back with them. They went as far as to tell him *'I will promote thee unto very great honour, and I will do whatsoever thou sayest unto me:*

Now this was right down Balaam's alley. But evidentially God instilled a slight fear into Balaam from the last time they spoke.

I would think that there is a difference in speaking or bringing up evil spirits and then getting to speak to the Lord God. There's got to be a difference in this. Balaam knew that the Living God came to him the first time concerning the Israelites. I'm sure there was a taste of fear in his mouth from that.

We see Balaam's response in verse 18- *'If Balak would give me his house full of silver and gold, I cannot go beyond the word of the LORD my God,'* I noticed here he refers to God as the LORD (Israel's God) as my God. I do not think that Balaam was now converted, but only realized that the LORD is the true and living God that came to him. We skip down to verse 20 and see that God said to him, if they call you to go, then go.

Then verse 21 Balaam went with the men. The next thing that happens is very strange unless you understand the will of God. We see in verse 22- *And God's anger was kindled because he went....*

Now why do you suspect that God allowed him to go then got mad because he went? I believe that had Balaam possessed a sincere spirit of obedience, he would have found in the first instructions, verse 12, a final decision upon the matter.

You see that God told him to start with, don't you go with those people. God does not approve of everything that he allows to go on. God is not pleased when men do the evil that He may permit. To deliberately and purposefully oppose the will of God is to make God your adversary.

Here is the second lesson we can learn from this story; there are times when you and I have a selfish will to go against God for whatever reason. God directly tells us no, whether it's from a passage in the Bible or by our conscience. But God has not given us approval upon the matter.

The point at which you follow your own lustful desires and disobey God is when you've just made God your adversary. We see this in verse 22. We need to realize the seriousness of disobedience. God isn't pleased with this.

Jumping ahead to chapter 23 Balaam told Balak; "that which God tells me I will relay it back to you." Three different times Balak showed Balaam the camp of the children of Israel and three times Balaam blessed the children of Israel. At the last mount Balaam saw the entire camp of the Israelites- 24:2-*And Balaam lifted up his eyes, and he saw Israel abiding in his tents according to their tribes....*

What he saw was a gigantic Cross! You see, when the children of Israel camped, they would split into their tribes. The ark/tabernacle in the center, three tribes to its east, west, north and south. This formed a huge cross., Anyone that may have seen the Israelites from on top of a hill would have seen the cross.

Balaam set out at the beginning of his journey to curse God's chosen people, but at the end gave a threefold blessing and then prophesied of the coming Prince of Israel.

The Bible tells us in 2 Peter 2:15-*which have forsaken the right way, and are gone astray, following the way of Balaam the son of Bosor, who loved the wages of unrighteousness;* Balaam was a false prophet that only wanted money, power, and luxury.

Despite his wickedness, God still used him to bless His people in front of Balak. The sad part of this whole story is that in the end, Balaam's counsel to Balak ended up turning the children of Israel to sin, promoting God's judgment.

We see this in Numbers 31:15, 16-*And Moses said unto them, Have you saved all the women alive? Behold, these caused the children of Israel, through the counsel of Balaam, to commit trespass against the Lord in the matter of Peor, and there was a plague among the congregation of the Lord.*

Balaam told Balak, don't use your men to fight against the children of Israel, but use your women to turn the children of Israel to fornication and to worship false idols, then God himself will pour wrath upon them. That is what Balak did and that is what happened to the Israelites.

We've now looked at the error of Balaam. His error was his love for money, power and fame. Secondly, it was his counsel of wickedness that sent the wrath of God after His chosen people.

You and I need to take heed to Jude's warning of not being deceived by the influences of this world. Money is only a tool. Power, when in subjection to the will of God is good, and fame, is fine when used to promote God and not your personal agenda.

Then we need to watch out for that wicked counsel that can sneak into the church though friends or family members that aren't saved or not right with God.

We have too much to lose as Christians to allow the error of Balaam to trip up our lives. Let's stay in the word and keep the right kind of influence in our lives.

We've seen the '**way of Cain**' and how he could care less about the things and laws of God. He believed that only his way was important. Cain's way led him to carelessly observe the offering of God. Cain's way led him to hate God and then to murder his own brother. Cain's way stripped him of his job, and his parents and caused him to roam the world as a vagabond with no place to call home, no one to call brother, and worst of all, no one that he was willing to call Lord.

When the dust had settled and the sentence was passed out, there was no remorse, no penitence, no grief over his own sin, nor the loss of his brother, only self-concern.

We saw Cain leave the face of God never to desire His presence again. Yes, Cain's way is the broad way, which many men have walked and I say many more will walk.

You and I know that way, his way, Cain; his way leads to damnation, misery, contempt, and utter loss. We know that Cain is in hell tonight, not because he murdered his brother, not because he gave a meager offering, but because he did not seek reconciliation with the Father of all living.

Next, we've looked at 'the error of Balaam' and how greed had cost this man his life. Not only his physical life, but also his spiritual life. His everlasting life was traded in for prosperity for wealth for the here today and gone tomorrow. Balaam had the chance to inherit this everlasting life. He was at the door of salvation, speaking directly to the One who offers it freely. But instead, he suffers everlasting death, pain and torments from the flames of hell.

I wonder how often he thinks to himself; if only. If only I listened to my God. If only I stayed and surrendered my life to the one who came to me by night.

I wonder how many men in the past have 'ran greedily after the error of Balaam for reward' not realizing the reward was only wood, hay and stubble, that would one day burn up in the flames of hell. If only.

If only, listen to me, don't you do it! Don't you read this book and think to yourself that it will be different for me. Don't think that God wont expect you to come to him with the plea of mercy. You'll wake up in hell before you could ever work your way into heaven. You'll wake up in hell before you could ever buy your way into heaven. Listen to me! Don't think for one minute that anything apart from the blood of Christ will ever get you one second of heaven.

You will fool yourself right into the devil's pit by believing that. Only what Christ has done will last for all eternity. Now with this in mind, let's finish this verse.

And perished in the gainsaying of Core- Perished means, *to be lost eternally; to be sentenced to endless misery.* Gainsaying means, *Contradicting; denying or opposing.* The story of Korah begins in the Old Testament book of Numbers Chapter 16:1-*Now Korah, the son of Izhar, the son of Kohath, the son of Levi, and Dathan and Abiram, the sons of Eliab, and On, the son of Peleth, sons of Reuben, took men:*

Did you notice the last two words of this verse? Right at the beginning of the chapter we see Korah teaming up with other men, the men named are Dathan and Abiram and On. but as we go further into this chapter, you will notice that this is the only time that On was ever mentioned. Most likely he stepped down from the rebellion realizing that he was fighting against God, and not man. At least we hope he realized this.

Who were these men? Who was Korah? He was a distant cousin to Moses and Aaron seen in Exodus 6:18. Then you have Dathan and Abiram. These men were sons of Eliab, which were sons of Reuben.

These men were not chosen by God to be priests. They had duties of course as all the Levites did. But theirs was not to do priestly things. Only a selected few from the tribe of Levi had that duty.

They took men, it said in verse two. There were *two hundred and fifty princes of the assembly, famous in the congregation, men of renown:* What's going on here? Why did Korah and these men rise up as its stated in verse two? We see the answer in verse three-...*ye take too much upon you, seeing all the congregation are holy, every one of them, and the LORD is among them: wherefore then lift ye up yourselves above the congregation of the LORD?*

What was Korah saying here? He was saying, hey Moses, you've gone too far, you're not the only holy person in this congregation, for we are all holy. You've lifted yourself up above us and that's wrong. You have no right to exalt yourself above the rest of us.

What a bold statement he made. God put Moses in the position that he was in, not Moses. God told Moses to lead His children. Moses was obeying God's will not his own.

But Korah didn't see it that way. Listen up, you know Korah grew up with the same knowledge of who Moses was along with everyone else. I'm sure he saw the miracles over in Egypt and walked through the Red Sea on dry ground, just like the rest of the Israelites. Why didn't he see the hand of God on Moses?

I believe it was because he had a corrupt heart and would not obey the command of God. Some people are like that. There are many people who know of God but could care less of God's word or His precautions on sin.

In verses 4-11 we see Moses response to Korah's accusation. *And when Moses heard it, he fell upon his face: And he spake unto Korah and unto all his company, saying, Even to morrow the Lord will shew who are his, and who is holy; and will cause him to come near unto him: even him whom he hath chosen will he cause to come near unto him. This do; Take you censers, Korah, and all his company; And put fire therein, and put incense in them before the Lord to morrow: and it shall be that the man whom the Lord doth choose, he shall be holy: ye take too much upon you, ye sons of Levi. And Moses said unto Korah, Hear, I pray you, ye sons of Levi: Seemeth it but a small thing unto you, that the God of Israel hath separated you from the congregation of Israel, to bring you near to himself to do the service of the tabernacle of the Lord, and to stand before the congregation to minister unto them? And he hath brought thee near to him, and all thy brethren the sons of Levi with thee: and seek ye the priesthood also? For which cause both thou and all thy company are gathered together against the Lord: and what is Aaron, that ye murmur against him?*

Did you see in verse four Moses' absolute humble attitude towards this situation? Moses knew God well enough to know that He doesn't put up with that kind of fool-doings.

Then in verse 5, he replied to Korah, *Even to morrow the LORD will shew who are his, and who is holy; and will cause him to come near unto him: even him whom he hath chosen will he cause to come near unto him.*

Look at what Paul said in 2 Timothy 2:19-*Nevertheless the foundation of God standeth sure, having this seal, the Lord knoweth them that are his. And, Let every one that nameth the name of Christ depart from iniquity.*

Paul knew that we won't buckle standing upon God's foundation, and his surety is His seal which says; *The Lord knoweth them that are his.* We don't have to compromise our faith, our convictions, our positions in Christ, when we stand with God.

Did you get that? When we stand with God-Moses already knew this, he told them, the Lord will show who are His and who is holy. Moses didn't have to defend himself, God would do it for him.

Now in verse 6 began the Authenticity Trial. It started by everyone involved taking a censer. A Censer *a container in which incense is burned, typically during a religious ceremony.* At verse 7- Moses declares that on the morrow- *"The man whom the Lord doth choose, he shall be holy:* The last part of verse 7, Moses declares *ye take too much upon you, ye sons of Levi.* This was aimed chiefly at Korah; for he was a Levite.

What exactly did Korah and the Levites do? What was their job and their inheritance? Over in Numbers 18:20-32 God told Aaron the following:

a. *Thou shalt have no inheritance in their land.*

b. *Neither shalt thou have any part among them.*

c. *I am thy part and thine inheritance among the children of Israel.*

d. *God gives the tenth of Israel for an inheritance, for their service which they serve, even for the service of the tabernacle of the congregation.*

e. *The Levites shall do the service of the tabernacle of the congregation.*

f. *They shall bear their iniquity.*

g. *They were to receive the tithe of the people, and then offer a tithe of that unto God.*

God had given the Levites a glorious reward, not land or material that would pass away but their reward would be Himself.

Numbers 18:20-*I am thy part and thine inheritance.* What more could one ask for? But Korah wasn't satisfied with God, he wanted the authority and the power that Moses had. Only he didn't realize the power Moses was given came from God. Only God could have given it to someone else.

In verses 8-10 Moses reminded Korah and the others of this. Look at what he said to them in verse 9-*Seemeth it but a small thing unto you, that the God of Israel hath separated you from the congregation of Israel, to bring you near to himself to do the service of the tabernacle of the Lord, and to stand before the congregation to minister unto them?*

Moses told them, do you think what God did for you was worthless? Is it not enough, that God is your inheritance-you were chosen to work the tabernacle, and to serve the Lord in the service of the tabernacle.

Verse 10-*...seek ye the priesthood also?* Moses asked; "you want Aaron's job also?" This was given to Aaron by God, not by man. Only God chose who became the priest or who performed the priestly duties.

In verse 12, things get heated up even more. *And Moses sent to call Dathan and Abiram, the sons of Eliab: which said, we will not come up:* These two, when requested by Moses, refused to listen to him. Then the next two verses give their bitter reasoning for their disobedience. Their complaint was that Moses allowed them to see the promise land yet not occupy it. They didn't remember the sins of their fathers who forsook God's command to take the land.

60

Their fathers refused to listen to Moses due to their unbelief and stated that there were giants in the land. Nevertheless, these two pointed all the blame to Moses.

Now in verse 15, Moses became angry and said to God *"respect not thou their offering"* Then he gave the test of who the Lord has called to lead. This is seen in verses 16-17. Let's. Look at the next few verses;

Verse 20-The Lord began to speak unto the congregation.

Verse 21-*Separate yourselves from among this congregation that I may consume them in a moment.* God was going to destroy the entire population, and He would have been just in doing so.

Verse 22-We see Moses and Aaron pleading with God for mercy.

Verse 24- God told them to separate the followers of Korah from the followers of God.

The next few verses Moses pleaded with the people to separate themselves from those wicked men. At this point the families of the wicked men came out of their tents;

Verse 28- Moses says *"hereby ye shall know that the Lord hath sent me to do all these works."*

Verse 29-30 Moses called for some new thing to happen so that the people will know that God judged these wicked men and not Moses and Aaron.

Verse 31-33- The earth swallowed those men and all that pertained to them.

Verse 34- the people fled.

Verse 35- God's Judgment was not through. The 250 men God burned with fire.

Verse 36-40- the Lord wanted Moses to have the censers taken from the dead and made into broad plates for a covering of the alter. This was to be done for a memorial. God is jealous of the honor of His own institutions and will not have them invaded. One commentator said;

The censors were devoted, so they must be serviceable to the glory of God.

-Matthew Henry

After all of this we still read in Numbers 26:11- *Notwithstanding the children of Korah died not.* This says a lot considering that the families of the other two men perished with them.

So, now we see how Korah didn't just get himself killed by his disobedience, but hundreds of others also. How many times have I heard of churches splitting because of one Korah, and countless lives die because of it? Do you understand this? Yes, souls die, people go to hell because Christians are too busy fussing and arguing with each other, and the Gospel message ceases to be sent out from that church.

Christians need to heed Jude's advice and not to go in the way of Cain. Meaning we should listen to God and obey His word. We shouldn't run greedily after the error of Balaam, meaning that we shouldn't follow money and worldly desires and lust. We should remember that God provides for us, and that is sufficient.

Thirdly we shouldn't listen to the gainsaying of Korah. He died, and took countless souls with him. I don't want to ever be on the side of God's wrath. His chastening hurts enough.

Today, if you have found yourself in the likeness of Cain, Balaam, or Korah, want you take some time and get it right with God. God wants you to be right with Him.

Jude 12-**These are spots in your feasts of charity, when they feast with you, feeding themselves without fear: clouds they are without water, carried about of winds; trees whose fruit withereth, without fruit twice dead plucked up by the roots;**

These are spots in your feasts of charity- The word spot is most likely a type of transliteration of the Greek word <u>spilas</u> meaning *a ledge or a reef or rock in the sea.* This means that a spot could be such as a false teacher, a flaw in truth, or a stigma.

The term '<u>feasts of charity</u>' means *goodwill, love benevolence.*

More so, of the love of person to person; especially of that love of Christians towards Christians which is enjoined and prompted by their religion, whether the love be viewed as in the soul or as expressed.

Jude began his description of these vial, wicked men with a nautical portrait. That first phrase stumped me to begin with; *These are spots in your feasts of charity.* It only became clear as I studied the Scripture.

Imagine with me the Christian life as a majestic vessel floating on the Atlantic sea. Your faith has spread its sails wide open allowing for the maximum flow of the wind to carry you on your journey of this Christian life. Smooth sailing, but wait, just like the deceitful reefs off the North Carolina coast, life's sea also has with its adventures, these unsuspecting reefs or spots.

Just when things were going your way, and life seems to be smooth sailing, you feel a bump, hear a screech, then the fearful noise of water leaking within your beautiful vessel. But wait a minute, your doing so well learning the Bible, being faithful to church. You've followed all the maps, listened to all the preaching, read your Bible daily. Why did this happen? These reefs weren't ever spoken about. They weren't here the last time you sailed this route. But, Satan has his pawns working hard to custom build that reef, especially for you.

It's no different for the newborn Christian. He's eager to break open his sails against the winds on life's sea. He feels the breeze catching his sails guiding his ship across the waves, its rough at first then once in the open sea, smooth sailing, for a little while.

But these spots, these reefs that the apostates strategically place in their path, waiting for the unsuspecting Christian to glide right over it, and once his ship hits it, his vessel is broken up, possibly lost upon the sea.

What happened? The new born Christian was opening up to the church. He was beginning to speak in Sunday school and ask questions. He started a reading program and bought a good study Bible.

I'll tell you what happened. This reef, that caused so much hurt, so much pain, and possibly caused this new born to quit on God, was an apostate. They come into the church, subtly spreading lies, and heresy. They question the pastor's message. They cause strife, they vent, or even teach flat out heresy in the church.

Most of the time, these new born Christians don't have the faith to rebuild their vessel, and they are captives on the island of bitterness. No, they didn't lose their salvation, but they lost the joy of their salvation, they lost the fervor of serving Christ.

That's why, my friend, we must be on a constant guard of who we put into offices of leadership. You are to pick a man of God to preach not a novice. Not someone that gives you an hour of personal illustrations and five minutes of Bible. Don't you do it. You need the sincere milk of the word of God, not a watered-down formula.

Your children need to be taught the word of God from their youth up. I have nothing against games and fun and eating, but Sunday mornings, Sunday nights are for the preaching of the word. Put your basketball up and get out the word of God, and expound on the word.

Most church kids have never heard a clear presentation of the gospel message. That's a shame. Shame on us if our children grow up in church and they never even once get convicted of their sin. Shame on us if we pop in a video of Christian cartoons in Sunday school instead of teaching them Bible. I have nothing against Christian cartoons, but it shouldn't take the place of Bible teaching.

Who are these apostates? Who are these that Jude spoke of? They may be sitting beside you in Sunday school, they may be a helper, they may sing specials, or sing in the choir. They are faithful, they lock up the buildings on Sundays. They stay after a special day to help clean up. Yes, these apostates don't mind getting their hands dirty if they can get your children's mind dirty in the process.

A false teacher can cause utter destruction upon a church. That's why it's important that we make sure that not only are we teaching Bible, but what about others in the church? We need to make sure our children are being taught the Scriptures properly. You know, most church splits can be avoided by a solid biblical Pastor, teaching the complete word of God. Then you must keep a thorough check on who becomes members, teachers, deacons and treasurers.

Some of you may say, "you mean we need to check people out before they become members?" yes. Would you let a couple become members if they are living together without being married? What if they were drug abusers? It's best to always make sure that potential members, not only know what the church believes and stands on but also what they believe in? What do they stand on and do they agree with the bi-laws of the church? Sad to say, most churches don't even speak to potential members until after they have joined. That's dangerous.

Don't take it lightly that you are a member of a local body of believers. You may not hold an office, but you do hold a vote, you do have a voice. Stand up for truth, don't give apostasy a chance to creep in.

When they feast with you, feeding themselves without fear- You partake of communion out of love, you get together with the brethren at the table to uplift each other and enjoy the fellowship. These apostates, wreak havoc while breaking bread. They only take of communion so as not to be noticed odd.

In Isaiah 56:11-*Yea, they are greedy dogs which can never have enough, and they are shepherds that cannot understand: they all look to their own way, every one for his gain, from his quarter.* The Bible calls these men greedy dogs, never able to fill their bellies. They are pastors that can never seem to preach truth, because they are void of knowledge, and the Spirit of God, looking only to their way as being the right way.

The Bible also tells us of these wicked men, like these apostate pastors in Ezekiel 34:8- *As I live, saith the Lord God, surely because my flock became a prey, and my flock became meat to every beast of the field, because there was no shepherd, neither did my shepherds search for my flock, but the shepherds fed themselves, and fed not my flock;*

God is not pleased with these pastors that feed themselves and not His sheep. As Jude said, *feeding themselves without fear.* The Bible gives us an example of this in Psalms 78:29- *So they did eat, and were well filled: for he gave them their own desire; They were not estranged from their lust. But while their meat was yet in their mouths, The wrath of God came upon them, and slew the fattest of them, and smote down the chosen men of Israel.*

Who are these verses referring to? What was going on here? Well, as so often in our Jude study, he takes us back to the Pentateuch. Let's look in the book of Numbers chapter 11.

Numbers 11:4-*and the mixt multitude that was among them fell a lusting: and the children of Israel also wept again, and said, Who shall give us flesh to eat?*

There is always a mixed multitude within the church, they are unsaved, they complain about everything. Toilet paper, carpet, temperature, grass, you name it they will complain about it. And what does that do?

...and the children of Israel also wept again.... This caused some of the Christian folk to start complaining. Not the ones who have been reading and studying their Bibles, but the Sunday Christians. These were the ones that were complacent and though they may be faithful to activities they weren't very committed in their relationship with God.

What was their complaint about? *Who shall give us flesh to eat?* They wanted meat to eat. Why? What was it they were eating that they weren't satisfied with?

Well, look with me at Exodus 16:14-15-*And when the dew that lay was gone up, behold, upon the face of the wilderness there lay a small round thing, as small as the hoar frost on the ground. And when the children of Israel saw it, they said one to another, it is manna: for they wist not what it was. And Moses said unto them, This is the bread which the LORD hath given you to eat.*

God, as always, provided them with food, bread from heaven, and the people called it manna. This manna was as small as a BB and they had to work to gather it, then grind it into a flour to cook it. God believes in working for your food.

So, in Numbers 11:5, they began to remember all the 'good times and good food' they enjoyed while slaves back in Egypt. In verse 6 the phrase *'but now our souls is dried away'* seems to mean that they have no more appetite for the manna, that they have to work so hard at preparing. In verse 10-the complaint was wide spread throughout the camp.

Now let's read verses 18-21- *And say thou unto the people, Sanctify yourselves against to morrow, and ye shall eat flesh: for ye have wept in the ears of the LORD, saying, Who shall give us flesh to eat? For it was well with us in Egypt: therefore the LORD will give you flesh, and ye shall eat. ye shall not eat one day, nor two days, nor five days, neither ten days, nor twenty days: But even a whole month, until it come out at your nostrils, and it be loathsome unto you: because that ye have despised the LORD which is among you, and have wept before him, saying, Why came we forth out of Egypt?*

God gave them their desire in verse 31. In hearing their complaints, their lust for something more than manna, God said you'll eat this flesh until you become disgusted with it, and long to never see it again.

Now in verses 21-23, Moses wondered how God would fulfill such a request as this, and said, there just isn't enough flesh, (herds or fish) to supply meat to this multitude. Moses' faith wavered some here.

Then we see God's answer in verse 23-...*Is the Lord's hand waxed short? Thou shalt see now whether my word shall come to pass unto thee or not.* God reminded Moses that He did have the power to do exactly what He said He would do. Today, God is indeed faithful to fulfill his promises whether they be promises of mercy or promises of wrath. God is faithful.

In verses 31-34, Massive amounts of quail came through the entire camp. Everyone was being fed, then in verse 33- *And while the flesh was yet between their teeth, ere it was chewed, the wrath of the Lord was kindled against the people, and the Lord smoke the people with a very great plague.*

What caused the Lord to become angry with the people? Look at verse 34-...*because there they buried the people that lusted.* The people craved meat and wasn't satisfied with the manna from God.

Just as Jude spoke that they were '*feeding themselves without fear*' Their belly was their god, and their flesh had to be satisfied, regardless of the consequences of their actions.

Paul said this in Philippians 3:19-*Whose end is destruction, whose God is their belly, and whose glory is in their shame, who mind earthly things.* Then James said in James 5:5-*Ye have lived in pleasure on the earth, and been wanton; Ye have nourished your hearts, as in a day of slaughter.* Paul also told us in 1 Thessalonians 5:6-*Therefore let us not sleep, as do others; but let us watch and be sober.*

Paul, like Jude said to watch, be sober, not to feed our belly with the lust of the flesh, but to live as Christians ought to, in line and accordance to God's word. Too many Christians are destroyed because they remain babies, never growing in the knowledge and love of Christ. Hosea said in 4:6-*My people are destroyed for lack of knowledge:*

Churches across America are teaching lies, and errors because the pastor doesn't know how to study the word, much less know how to teach it to his people. Errors in doctrine get passed down from generation to generation because no one wants to do the work of studying anymore.

Yes, it's hard work, but it's also a rewarding work. Jude said that these hidden rocks, these reefs, they are out there and can destroy your life. You must be on a constant guard to protect yourself, your family, and your church. Don't be a casualty on life's sea.

How does one keep apostasy from entering the church? First by knowing what the Bible says, and understanding what it says. For too long now, our churches have been getting their ears tingled as Paul warned Timothy. For too long now, American pastors have been giving their flock five minutes of Bible and forty-five minutes of personal illustrations, stories and humor.

The problem is that most of the congregation enjoys story time more than they enjoy the opening of Scripture and expounding upon it. We've lost it in our churches. We've lost the desire to hear God's word being preached.

We've lost our hunger for the word of God. We've starved ourselves in the churches for so long, and have forgotten what the pure undiluted word of God sounds like!

We need to get back to some pure preaching of the Bible. I don't care if the preacher hollers or is soft spoken, so long as he preaches the entire word. I need to hear the word preached, not anything less.

Clouds they are without water, carried about of winds- What was Jude trying to tell us in this passage? *Clouds they are without water, ...* I am reminded of what Paul told the Ephesians in chapter 4:14-*That we henceforth be no more children, tossed to and fro, and carried about with every wind of doctrine, by the sleight of men, and cunning craftiness, whereby they lie in wait to deceive;*

How does a man, who believes that he is called of God, how does he start out on the right path of truth and knowledge, only to end up becoming an apostate? It's not an overnight process. It takes months, even years to warp a man's mind into believing a lie. It begins by Satan planting that seed of doubt into one's heart.

A person might start off with a book given to him by a friend, quite possibly the book is 95 percent truth, with only 5 percent error. But that five percent is enough to sway a weak mind.

That's why you shouldn't only guard your children on what they read, but guard yourself also. I only read from people that I trust. Meaning, if I know the book or author is ok, then I will read that person's work.

Allow me to give you a good rule to live by; never read an author that you haven't been introduced to by way of reference. If a more spiritual Christian than you hasn't recommend it to you, or another author that you trust

68

references it in their book, then chances are you shouldn't read them. You can always ask your pastor or mentor if they've heard of that book or author. Get advice before you read someone unfamiliar.

Paul said here in Ephesians that, *we henceforth be no more children*. We need to stop being baby Christians and grow up. Some of us have been saved for 20 plus years, and still haven't read the Bible from cover to cover. You still don't have a solid prayer life; you still don't have a decent Christian testimony. GROW UP, Paul said.

Then Paul said; *tossed to and fro, and carried about with every wind of doctrine*. First, and I know that I am repeating myself, but I can't stress this enough; guard what you read.

Second; guard what you listen to. While you may guard your eyes, you will also need to guard your ears. Don't just listen to every preacher that's on the radio. If you happen to come across someone preaching whom you're not familiar with, turn it off. It's better to wait and ask someone that you respect as a seasoned Christian if they ever heard of a certain preacher, and what they know about that person. We need to guard our ears to what is being played on the radio.

That also goes for revival services. If you don't know the speaker, then find out who they are and what they stand for. You're better off not going, then to go and take your family with you and get caught up in error.

Paul concluded this verse with; *by the sleight of men, and cunning craftiness, whereby they lie in wait to deceive;* The number one goal of the apostate is to deceive the believer. If Satan can get you to stumble in your faith, then he has started you on the path of quitting or becoming an apostate yourself.

That term the slight of men simply means *the subtlety or trickery of men.* This is Satan's favorite tool against God's people. It doesn't happen overnight but over a period. We are often duped into apostasy; we're fooled into believing a lie. How does this happen to Christians? because most Christians are ignorant of God's Word.

Too many Christians believe that just going to church is good enough to get them through life. It's a good start but not enough. Jude told his readers and he is telling us today not to fall into the trap of false teaching. That's why we need to be consistent in reading the word of God and in studying it.

Don't fall into the trap of deception. Don't fall into Satan's lies by one of his pawns. Know what your Bible says, learn the truth, know who God is and what He expects from His people. Don't get caught up in the latest fads of religion.

Trees whose fruit withereth, without fruit, twice dead, plucked up by the roots- Jude was saying that these apostates were spiritually dead, they produced no fruit for God's kingdom and since they were spiritually dead, their second death will be in hell. For they rejected the Savior as their substitute for the second death, by which, they could have received eternal life.

John told us in his gospel, chapter 15, starting in verse 4-*Abide in me, and I in you.* This is a command, not a suggestion. Too many Christians don't know what it means to abide in Christ.

Here, the word abide means *to bear patiently, to endure.* We are to bear our life's burden patiently in Christ.

Here is the entire verse of John 15:4-*Abide in me, and I in you. As the branch cannot bear fruit of itself, except it abide in the vine; no more can ye, except ye abide in me.*

In today's Christian circle, the reason we can't take hard times, and we can't produce any of the fruit of the Spirit is because we don't obey Christ when He says to "abide in me."

When we're not completely satisfied with the love of Christ in our life, we will quit abiding. That's when we become unhappy, and we become miserable in this life and we wander along aimlessly without any guidance.

Start abiding in Christ once again and you can regain your love for God. The apostates that Jude was speaking of were not abiding in Christ, they weren't part of his branches, and that is why they weren't bearing fruit.

Jude warned us of preachers, pastors, and teachers whose number one objective is to destroy the church. Our job as true Christians is to make sure that doesn't happen at our church. You have a duty to protect your church.

Now what happens in another church is their business. One thing more Christians need to learn is to keep our noses out of other churches affairs. This doesn't mean we need to condone their error. We don't have to condone everything that other churches do. But, we are to stay out of their business.

If a church teaches error, I wouldn't go and try to fix it, because it's none of my business what they teach. I wouldn't condone their behavior; neither would I accept their beliefs. But it's none of my business what their pastor preaches behind his pulpit. That is between them and God. But you and I could pray for them. Pray that God would show them their error before it's too late.

I believe that too many Christians have fallen victim of thinking it's their job to point out the errors of other churches and then making it their business to try and correct them or drag their name in the mud.

I don't mind pointing out the errors of churches for illustrations but I will not name names. That I believe is going too far, for like I said, I believe that to each church they stand or fall before God on their merits. They don't give an account to me on what they do.

If there comes a day that you must look for another church home, it will be your duty to find one that will teach truth, and not apostasy. I hope that you will be up to the task. Make sure that you take a stand on biblical principles.

Throughout Jude we've been hearing about apostates and how they creep into churches and devour its members. How can this be except that they can mimic; the look, talk and act of other true believers?

No doubt that there are apostates that to you and I would never suspect them of being anything other than a Christian. How do we point these apostates out? by knowing God's word and rightly dividing the word of truth. Nothing hard about it, except that most Christians are too lazy to study their Bible to learn what to look for.

Next most Christians don't get enough Bible preached to them behind the pulpit for them to learn the word while at church. We are in a sad state in America, because of our churches.

Jude 13-**Raging waves of the sea, foaming out their own shame; wandering stars, to whom is reserved the blackness of darkness for ever.**

Raging waves of the sea- In this verse, Jude continued his picture of what these apostates are like. I picture in my mind an ocean, angry that a vessel is floating upon her. She strives tossing the vessel to and fro upon the waves, dashing herself relentlessly on the sides of the vessel.

The word raging means *furious; vehemently driven or agitated.* These raging waves describe the apostates, the same ones who *have gone in the way of Cain, and ran greedily after the error o Balaam for reward, and perished in the gain saying of Core.*

No shame, no morals have ever been linked with them. They show no fear of God much less respect for Him. Though they may be in leadership positions, and even a pastor or teacher, the truth is not in them. They can't teach truth, for the Spirit of truth isn't in them. The only signs of growth are that of a cancerous disease and it only brings forth death.

Isaiah told us in 57:20-*But the wicked are like the troubled sea, when it cannot rest, whose waters cast up mire and dirt.* Did you catch the similarities of this verse and what Jude spoke of?

The wicked are like the troubled sea, and Jude said that these apostates are as the Raging waves of the sea. They are also wicked, that word wicked means *persons who live in sin; transgressors of the divine law; all who are unreconciled to God, unsanctified or impenitent.*

Jude called the apostates, wicked and rightfully so, for they are the ones who stir up the waters. But allow me to remind you of the one who can calm the raging sea. Psalms 65:7-*Which stilleth the noise of the seas, the noise of their waves, and the tumult of the people.* They may rage as the sea sometimes does, they may make noise of tumult but Christ has power over the seas, He has power over these lost men and women who try to overcome His church.

That's why it's important that we allow Him to work in our church, allow Him the freedom to move freely within the local church.

It also says in Psalms 93:3,4-*The floods have lifted up, O LORD, the floods have lifted up their voice: the floods lift up their waves. The LORD on high is mightier than the noise of many waters, yea, than the mighty waves of the sea.*

Again, the Psalmist reminded us that God is mightier than the ocean, though we can see the waves beat down upon us, the wind blowing us around and fill the chill of the waters' temperature; God created the waves, the wind and the temperature. His might is unparalleled to anything Satan may use against us here on this earth.

So, let the storms come upon the sea, let the winds howl, let the waves roar her mighty voice, because it's only within God's will that these things are so. God is, and has always been in control.

Have you personally noticed in your own life that you've forgotten that God is in control? If so, I want to remind you that God has not forgotten about you or what you're going through. He has your hand. Now let Him lead.

Foaming out their own shame- Foaming means *to cast out as foam (Jude called the godless and graceless set of whom he spoke, impelled by their restless passions, they unblushingly exhibit, in word and deed, their base and abandoned spirit.)* This word shame means *shameful deeds.* Paul spoke of this in Philippians 3:18,19 ***(For many walk, of whom I have told you often, and now tell you even weeping, that they are the enemies of the cross of Christ: Whose end is destruction, whose God is their belly, and whose glory is in their shame, who mind earthly things.)***

Paul said that these are the enemies of the cross of Christ, their end is Hell, their God is their belly, and they glory in their shame.

Why would someone glory in their shame? I've seen this before in my life. I'm sure you have too. These shameful deeds can be open sin, that you and I see in public.

I couldn't count the times I've seen drunks in public, acting a fool. Homosexuals displaying affection in public. I've been to countless houses where the couples aren't married, but are openly living together.

These are types of foaming out their own shame. This is distasteful to our Lord and it should also be distasteful to you and I. Paul warned us in 2 Timothy 3:13-***But evil men and seducers shall wax worse and worse, deceiving, and being deceived.***

This verse isn't speaking of the times becoming worse and worse, but the individual's themselves becoming worse and worse. Until they are completely and utterly vial as Satan himself.

These men continually burn in their own lust, filling their Bellies with wickedness until they are completely yoked with Satan and his work.

Wandering stars- What do we know about stars? scientist tells us that there could be as many as 100 octillion stars. That's a 1 with 29 zeros behind it. The Bible says in Psalms 147:4-*He telleth the number of stars; he calleth them all by their names.*

Well, first, we see that God counts (telleth) the stars. We have an awesome God that can count the stars. How does He do this? because He created them. In Psalm 19:1-*The heavens declare the glory of God; and the firmament sheweth his handywork.*

Have you ever looked up at the sky on a clear night and saw the stars twinkling above you? This is the handiwork of God. God is showing us what He can do. What a marvelous sight to behold.

But what was Jude speaking of in this verse when he said *wandering stars*? Was he speaking of literal stars or was this a figurative language spoken? I think that if we look at Revelation 12:3-4, it will help in explaining this part of the verse;

Revelation 12:3, 4-*And there appeared another wonder in heaven; and behold a great red dragon, having seven heads and ten horns, and seven crowns upon his heads. And his tail drew the third part of the stars of heaven, and did cast them to the earth: and the dragon stood before the woman which was ready to be delivered, for to devour her child as soon as it was born.*

In verse four John said that this dragon's tail drew the third part of the stars of heaven, and did cast them to the earth. Now from what I've studied, I do believe that John was speaking of Satan when referring to the great red dragon, and the third of the stars would be the fallen angels that leagued with him at the rebellion.

Jude spoke of wandering stars, possibly these false teachers, like the fallen angels, have no set orbit to which they are guided by, but wander from one false teaching to another, anything they can do to confuse, hinder, and put doubt upon the gospel while they are on this planet. But why? Jude finished by saying;

To whom is reserved the blackness of darkness forever- The same end and utter destruction is awaiting the false teachers as is awaiting these fallen angels, these fallen stars. The word blackness means *murky, appalling gloom, referring to darkness so dense and foreboding it is 'felt.'* The word darkness means *obscurity; figuratively-the principle of sin with its certain results.*

Peter said in 2 Peter 2:17-*These are wells without water, clouds that are carried with a tempest; to whom the mist of darkness is reserved for ever.*

Ever since the fall of the third part of the angelic host, there has been a coming judgment with a hefty sentence awaiting them. Hell, made originally for Satan and his angels, is a place of total darkness. Peter reminded us of this also.

2 Peter 2:4-*For if God spared not the angels that sinned, but cast them down to hell, and delivered them into chains of darkness, to be reserved unto judgment.*

This place of darkness, this hell, yes it was meant for the fallen angels and Satan, but now it has been enlarged to hold those that are lost without Christ.

Look at Isaiah 5:14-*Therefore hell hath enlarged herself, and opened her mouth without measure: and their glory, and their multitude, and their pomp, and he that rejoiceth, shall descend into it.* These apostates that go about causing confusion, lying, and deceiving people, they have a place in hell that awaits them.

Trust me, God's judgment will be heavy upon them for their evil deeds. You see, these deceivers appear to be Christians, while they continue to seduce, and tear down churches. They are just like their master, Satan. For Satan appears as an angel of light, to fool others, into thinking he is someone that he isn't.

Isaiah 14:12-*How art thou fallen from heaven, O Lucifer, son of the morning! How art thou cut down to the ground, which didst weaken the nations!* Isaiah went on to tell us what Satan said;

1. I will ascend into heaven,

2. I will exalt my throne above the stars of God

3. I will sit also upon the mount of the congregation, in the sides of the north:

4. I will ascend above the heights of the clouds;

5. I will be like the Most High.

He tried then and still continues to imitate the Most High, yet he is flawed. Though many times people are duped into believing his lies. His false teachers do the same thing, no new tricks just the same old ones, why? Because they still work.

If I said it once, I have said it a thousand times, Christians today don't know enough of the word of God to know heresy from the truth. It's as simple as that.

In the verse, we just read, it says *O Lucifer, son of the morning!* For some reason, Isaiah gave Satan a proper name; Lucifer. In the Hebrew, it is Halal meaning *a shining one.*

I am reminded of Revelation 22:16-*I Jesus have sent mine angel to testify unto you these things in the churches. I am the root and the offspring of David, and the bright and morning star.*

Satan's ambition has always been to be like the Most High. We've seen Isaiah's testimony of this in his book. Christ is our Bright and Morning Star. While Satan is a shining one, he isn't a bright star, only gives the appearance of a bright object.

Likewise, with his apostates. These men spoken about in Jude, they aren't teachers of the gospel of Christ, but teachers of Satan's gospel of hell and damnation.

They can't teach the things of God, but only try to come as close as they can to appear to be teachers of "light." But we know that they are mockers, and deceivers.

They have only one goal and that is to pull as many men, women and children to hell with them as they possibly can. Don't be fooled by their evil ways.

We need to know what our Bible says about doctrine. Just because a man walks around with a Bible in his hand does not make him a preacher nor does it make him a Christian. It's not what you carry in your hand, but what you carry in your heart that counts. Did you get that? Each church is only one pastor away from turning into an apostate church.

The choice you make could either make or break your church. Know your Bible, know your doctrine, and know the principles, and heart of the man of God you put behind the pulpit. It is your decision, I can't make it for you. You make sure that he is genuine and that you treat him like he deserves to be treated.

In this section, we've covered Jude speaking of these men as raging waves, foaming out their own shame. They don't care about you nor God.

Their concern is for their own lust and their own objectives. He also stated that their end is darkness forever. Just as the fallen angels, these men are promised eternal Hell and damnation. Let me ask you this; are you sure that if you were to die today that you would go to heaven? If not, take some time and make sure that you know you're going to heaven when you die.

Jude 14-**And Enoch also, the seventh from Adam, prophesied of these, saying, Behold, the Lord cometh with ten thousands of his saints,**

The story of Enoch begins in Genesis chapter five. Here are verses 18-24, *And Jared lived an hundred sixty and two years, and he begat Enoch: And Jared lived after he begat Enoch eight hundred years, and begat sons and daughters: And Enoch lived sixty and five years, and begat Methuselah: And Enoch walked with God after he begat Methuselah three hundred years, and begat sons and daughters: And all the days of Enoch were three hundred sixty and five years: And Enoch walked with God: and he was not; for God took him.*

When one reads these verses in Genesis, it's always hard to pass up the miracle of Enoch skipping over the grave and being transformed never to feel the sting of death.

Of course, this is indeed a miracle. But, I'm not so sure that this is what God wanted us to get out of these few verses. Yes, he was the first man, one of only two, that we know of, to never have died; Elijah being the other. But I personally believe that the more important issue is, what does the Bible say about Enoch while he was here on this earth? That is what we are going to look at. Also, we will look into the contrast of the two lines that came from Adam.

And Enoch also, the seventh from Adam- John Phillips said in his commentary- *Jude uses Enoch to contrast Cain, Balaam, and Korah. Those three men were the great apostates of their age; Enoch was the great apostle of his. Korah went to hell; Enoch went to heaven. Cain went his own way and became a stranger and vagabond on the earth; Enoch walked with God and became a pilgrim and a stranger on the earth but a citizen of heaven. Balaam loved gold; Enoch loved God.* - (Taken from Exploring the Epistle of Jude © Copyright 2004 by John Phillips. Published by Kregel Publications, Grand Rapids, MI. Used by permission of the publisher. All rights reserved.)

Adam and Eve gave birth to Cain and Abel after their fall and exit from the Garden of Eden. We know the story of how Cain slew his brother Abel in the field. So afterwards Cain left the presence of God not to be seen again.

Now, we see that after the death of Abel, that Adam and Eve had Seth. And in *Genesis 4:25-...and she bare a son, and called his name Seth: For God, said she, hath appointed me another seed instead of Abel, whom Cain slew.*

Then look at verse 26-*And to Seth, to him also there was born a son; and he called his name Enos: then began men to call upon the name of the LORD.*

That last phrase-*then began men to call upon the name of the LORD.* The lineage of Seth has often been called the godly line. This phrase right here is why. Adam and Eve knew that at the loss of Abel there was also a second loss. That was Cain. Eve knew that Cain left the presence of the Lord, never to return. So, when she gave birth to Seth she said, *God...hath appointed me another seed instead of Abel....*

This line, this godly line is the line that Enoch came from. You see, his daddy taught him about God and his daddy before him taught him. All the way back to Adam.

Prophesied of these, saying- What was Jude speaking of here? Rather who was Enoch prophesying of? Apostates! He was warning them of the apostates that were in the past, present and coming future!

Behold, the Lord cometh with ten thousands of his saints- Was Enoch speaking of the flood? No. Christ had not come, let alone ten-thousands of his saints. Was Enoch speaking of the birth of Christ? No. While on earth Isaiah said of him that *He is despised and rejected of men: a man of sorrows, and acquainted with grief: and we hid as it were our faces from him; he was despised, and we esteemed him not.*

No, Enoch wasn't speaking of the birth of Christ. Nor did He at that time have ten-thousands of saints, our Lord had only a handful of close disciples.

No, Enoch was speaking of the return of our Lord, when He comes to judge, as seen in 2 Thessalonians 1:7-8, *and to you who are troubled rest with us, when the Lord Jesus shall be revealed from heaven with his mighty angels, in flaming fire taking vengeance on them that know not God, and that obey not the gospel of our Lord Jesus Christ.*

What was Enoch's prophesy? It was a warning of the coming judgment of Christ the King of kings! And Lord of lords! In 1Thessalonians 3:13-*to the end he may stablish your hearts unblameable in holiness before God, even our father, at the coming of our Lord Jesus Christ with all his saints:*

See this isn't the rapture but the second coming of the Lord. He will execute Judgment upon the earth at that time.

Jude 15-**To execute judgment upon all and to convince all that are ungodly among them of all their ungodly deeds which they have ungodly committed, and of all their hard speeches which ungodly sinners have spoken against him.**

To execute judgment upon all- In Psalms 9:7,8 it says; *but the Lord shall endure for ever: he hath prepared his throne for judgment. And he shall judge the world in righteousness, he shall minister judgment to the people in uprightness.* The psalmist echoes the sermon that Enoch preached to his generation.

Who was this generation that he preached to? Well, if Enoch was the seventh from Adam in the line of Seth; then who was the seventh from Adam in the line of Cain? Do we know?

We see the answer to this question in Genesis 4:18b-*and Methuselah begat Lamech.* What do we know about this distant cousin of Enoch?

To find the answer to this question, let's look at verses 19-24; *And Lamech took unto him two wives: the name of the one was Adah, and the name of the other Zillah. And Adah bare Jabal: he was the father of such as dwell in tents, and of such as have cattle. And his brother's name was Jubal: he was the father of all such as handle the harp and organ. And Zillah, she also bare Tubal-Cain, an instructor of every artificer in brass and iron: and the sister of Tubal-Cain was Naamah. And Lamech said unto his wives, Adah and Zillah, hear my voice; Ye wives of Lamech, hearken unto my speech: for I have slain a man to my wounding, and a young man to my hurt. If Cain shall be avenged sevenfold, truly Lamech seventy and sevenfold.*

Ok, what do we see in these verses? The very first thing I would like to point out is that Lamech was the first man to take two wives. Now think with me here, was Lamech of the godly line of Seth or of the lost line of Cain? Cain, so what do you think God thought of a man taking two wives? Though a lot of godly men made this same mistake, it wasn't what God's intention was as far as marriage is concerned.

Moving on, what do we see about the children of Lamech?

1. Jabal was the father of herdsmen. Jabal fathered the law of supply and demand by domesticating animals and supplying them to the people who may have needed them.

80

2. Jubal was the father of the musical instruments. He pioneered the culture and refinement of the land, by supplying entertainment to the masses.

3. Tubal-Cain was the father of working with metals. Tubal-Cain pioneered the industrial revolution of that day, modernizing the people into a higher culture.

What was the world like in Enoch's day? Eat drink and be merry. Live comfortably make money, be happy. God was not on the top ten in their bucket list. I am reminded of Acts 17:30-31*And the times of this ignorance God winked at; but now commandeth all men every where to repent: because he hath appointed a day, in the which he will judge the world in righteousness by that man whom he hath ordained: whereof he hath given assurance unto all men, in that he hath raised him from the dead.*

I often wonder if they were truly ignorant of God or if they, like today's generation, choose to ignore God. Either way, Enoch preached to them the coming judgment.

And to convince all that are ungodly among them of all their ungodly deeds which they have ungodly committed- Did you notice that the word "ungodly" was used three times here in this section of the verse? Ungodly means *wicked, sinful, neglecting the fear and worship of God, or violating his commands.*

Jude was pointing out to his readers that these people weren't just decent lost folks who needed to be saved. No, they were vile in their horrible acts. Not only were they sinful, but they could care less about the commands and worship of God Almighty.

Paul said in Romans 2:5 & 6-*But after thy hardness and impenitent heart treasurest up unto thyself wrath against the day of wrath and revelation of the righteous judgment of God; Who will render to every man according to his deeds:*

I'm sure this was what Enoch preached and prophesied about. He told the people of their hard heart and their impenitent heart, which means *not repenting of sin.*

He warned them of how they were storing up a multitude of wrath against the day of God's judgment and how that Christ would one day deal His wrath out to every man according to his deeds.

Paul also said in Romans 3:19&20-*Now we know that what things so ever the law saith, it saith to them who are under the law: that every mouth may be stopped, and all the world may become guilty before God. Therefore by the deeds of the law there shall no flesh be justified in his sight: for by the law is the knowledge of sin.*

Some would argue that Enoch lived before the law of Moses. True, but God as we have seen in the beginning of Genesis, has always had a law for man to live by; to obey. Adam and Eve had their law, which they could not keep. So did the people of Enoch's day. God is a God of order, and we must realize that even though we may not see or have the written laws that were being abused in Enoch's time, God's commands were still being broken and abused, regardless. This was Enoch's message, "REPENT, for the Lord is prepared to Judge us."

And of all their hard speeches which ungodly sinners have spoken against him- The Psalmist said it spot on in Chapter 94:1-4, *O Lord God, to whom vengeance belongeth; O God to whom vengeance belongeth, shew thyself. Lift up thyself, thou judge of the earth: render a reward to the proud. Lord, how long shall the wicked, how long shall the wicked triumph? How long shall they utter and speak hard things? And all the workers of iniquity boast themselves?*

What was Enoch saying concerning these hard speeches? He was saying the exact thing the Psalmist said here. These wicked men women and children were blasphemous, irreverent, against God, His truth and His ways. As one commentator put it;

> *They laughed at Enoch and his God. They mocked him, mocked his ways and mocked at his love for them. How do I know that Enoch loved them? because he was warning them.*

So, who was this Enoch? Not much has ever been said about him. But we do know that he was called of God to preach and warn the people of his generation. We know that he obeyed God, we know that he walked with God, and we know that he was not, for God took him, meaning, he never saw death.

No, as amazing as his translation from earth to heaven was, what's more amazing is the life he lived while on this earth. Jude told us of Enoch's job here on earth, how that amongst the wicked he preached, and loved, and urged his friends and others to repent, but it looks like not many people ever listened to him.

As a preacher, it's not my job to convert, that's God's job. My job is to obey God by preaching His Word, in its absolute truth.

Jude has been giving us verse after verse of a complete description of what an apostate looks like. We've covered many descriptions, and will cover more. Now we will look at some of their actions, how they display themselves in the church.

You must always be on guard. Jude made it clear that you must know your enemy. Ignorance within the church, will kill the church. Some of us have been saved for ten or twenty or even more years than that. There is no excuse for us not to know a wolf when they enter the sheep fold.

Jude 16-**These are murmurers, complainers, walking after their own lust; and their mouth speaketh great swelling words, having men's persons in admiration because of advantage.**

These are murmurers, complainers- The meaning of <u>murmur</u> is *to grumble; to complain. So, a murmurer would be, one who grumbles, and/or complains.* The Psalmist spoke of the children of Israel in 106:21-26-*They forgat God their savior, which had done great things in Egypt; Wondrous works in the land of Ham, and terrible things by the Red Sea. Therefore he said that he would destroy them, had not Moses his chosen stood before him in the breach, to turn away his wrath, lest he should destroy them. Yea, they despised the pleasant land, they believed not his word: But murmured in their tents, and hearkened not unto the voice of the LORD. Therefore he lifted up his hand against them, to overthrow them in the wilderness:*

Often whenever we read the account of the children of Israel wandering around in the wilderness, we can see the endless cycle of them relying on God for deliverance or support. Then they become contempt with God and His goodness. Next, they start complaining about their situation and then they begin to sin.

We see that and we think to ourselves; "No! Wait! Stop before it's too late!" Even more so, we might even judge them, thinking, "why didn't you learn your lesson the last time you fell into sin?"

We never realize that we too are as guilty of the continual cycle of reliance upon God, contempt with God, complaining about God, then sinking head deep into our own sinful desires. The full story of this account is over in Deuteronomy chapter one.

The first few chapters of Deuteronomy cover the history of the Israelites while wandering around in the wilderness. And in chapter one we see the story of what Scofield called; "The failure at Kadesh-Barnea."

In Deuteronomy 1:26, 27-*Notwithstanding ye would not go up, but rebelled against the commandment of the LORD your God: And ye murmured in your tents, and said, Because the LORD hated us, he hath brought us forth out of the land of Egypt, to deliver us into the hand of the Amorites, to destroy us.*

This was Moses speaking unto the congregation reminding them of the events that he dealt with forty years ago with their fathers. He reminded them of how God had prepared a land for them to inherit, all they were to do was cross the river Jordan, and God would fight for them. Thus, giving them the land.

Moses had 12 spies to go out not to evaluate the land to see if it was conquerable but to see which direction to take, and what blessings awaited them on the other side Jordan. But when the spies came back, what did they give the people? They gave them some of the bountiful fruit of the land, but they also gave them an evil report.

They told the people, that there were giants in the land, and the cities had huge walls around them. They said that they were no match for them. They forgot that God was their deliverer, that God would fight the battles. They didn't have the faith to believe that God could.

So, what did they do? They began to complain. Moses said that they murmured in their tents, saying *"because the LORD hated us, he hath brought us forth out of the land of Egypt, to deliver us into the hand of the Amorites, to destroy us."*

They just witnessed the strong hand of God delivering them out of the Egyptian bondage! They witnessed the plagues that poured out on their captors. They witnessed the parting of the Red Sea and then the drowning of Pharaoh's army. For what reason did they have to doubt God?

Why do people begin to murmur? Simple, they believe that they are not getting what they deserve. Do you know what you and I deserve? Hell, pain, torment, poverty, heartache, all the above. The reason we are alive today and not in a grave is because of the mercy of God.

We forget all too often that God is a God of mercy. We forget that we are sinners deserving of the worst possible place in hell imaginable. If we are not careful we too could easily be mistaken for these apostates that Jude was speaking of.

When was the last time you caught, yourself complaining? Recently? All of us are guilty of it. But we must remember that God doesn't approve of it nor does He stand for it. This verse continues by saying;

Walking after their own lusts- The definition of <u>walking</u> in Scripture is *to live and act or behave; to pursue a particular course of life*. So, Jude said that these apostates were pursuing their own lusts, they lived and acted and behaved after their own lusts. What does the Bible tell us of this?

The Bible says in Galatians 5:16-*This I say then, walk in the Spirit, and ye shall not fulfill the lust of the flesh.* Do you think that these apostates that Jude referred to were fulfilling the lust of their flesh? Of course! They pursued their fleshly lust daily. Not ever concerned with the lifestyle of the godly. They couldn't walk in the Spirit because they didn't have the Spirit in them.

Verse twenty-five of this chapter in Galatians says; *If we live in the Spirit, let us also walk in the Spirit.* What was Paul saying here? How does one know if they are living in the Spirit? Well there is one solid way of knowing if you are living in the Spirit. Have you been born again? Simple as that. Have you been born again?

If you have, then you are living in, not your spirit, but the Holy Spirit lives within you and therefore you are living in His Spirit, hence, we live in the Spirit.

Paul was explaining that since you and I live with the presence of the Holy Spirit within us, then it's only right for you and I to walk in the presence of the Holy Spirit.

Why would we want to have the Holy Spirit's presence with us continually and then live our lives like we are hell bound? It doesn't make since. We should have a desire to walk in the Spirit, meaning we should pursue a godly Christian lifestyle that is acceptable to God the Father.

As Christ, our example, often said while on this earth, "not my will Father, but thine be done." Paul also warned us of these types of apostates in 2 Timothy 4:3-*For the time will come when they will not endure sound doctrine; but after their own lusts shall they heap to themselves teachers, having itching ears;*

What did Paul mean by this verse? Did he mean that in the end times, these things will happen? No, he meant in Timothy's time, and in our own time. Each generation must battle these apostates, until the end of times.

More and more will these apostates gather unto themselves false teachers, becoming vain in their own false doctrine. That term having <u>itching ears</u> means *that they want to hear something that is pleasing to their seared conscious.*

They don't want the Biblical messages, they want the 'feel good everything is gonna be alright' messages. Today, don't be fooled by these preachers that don't preach the entire Bible. They are more worried about crowds and money than your soul.

Can this happen to you? Are you exempt from becoming a false teacher or an apostate? Do you have it in you to stay faithful until the end? I sure hope so.

In James 1:14-*But every man is tempted, when he is drawn away of his own lust, and enticed. Then when lust hath conceived, it bringeth forth sin: and sin, when it is finished, bringeth forth death.* What does the book of James tell us about lust?

When are we tempted? When we are drawn away of our own lust, and enticed.

Ok, here is the scenario; we are walking after the things of God. Walking in His will and guided by the Holy Spirit. Out of nowhere, at the corner of our eye we spot sin, not just any sin, our own special recipe of sin. You know the one that so easily besets you and I. What do we do? Keep straight down the narrow path? We should, but no. We veer off towards that bright shiny package with our name on the ribbon.

What just happened? Have we sinned? No, but we are well on the way. We've just allowed lust to conceive, and this is what brings about sin, and as always, sin when it is finished, brings about death. We must remember that we are not above sin.

And their mouth speaketh great swelling words- What did he mean by this? Was this their preaching, or their conversation? Over in Jude's sister book, Peter, we see in 2 Peter 2:18-*For when they speak great swelling words of vanity, they allure through the lusts of the flesh, through much wantonness, those that were clean escaped from them who live in error.*

These teachers, preachers and false prophets spoke, whether behind the pulpit or one on one, with fluff, to make them feel like they were special. They lied, they twisted the Word and said anything so that the Christians would feel like somebody. Peter said here in this verse, "those that were clean escaped from them who live in error."

Those of us trying to live a clean life, we're in no position to give someone like this 5 seconds of our time. We must stay away from those who are always feeding others a bunch of fluff. Remember that those who daily remind themselves, the only good thing about them is the Lord God, they will keep themselves from these wicked people. Then finally this verse ends with;

Having men's persons in admiration because of advantage- Ok, let me first say that when reading this passage, I had no idea what Jude was talking about. But, that's why I study, I look up words, I read commentaries, I cross reference and compare Scripture with Scripture. Because I want to know what God has for us in His word.

While studying, I found a verse in Leviticus that really sheds some light on this passage. Leviticus 19:15-*Ye shall do no unrighteousness in judgment: thou shalt not respect the person of the poor, nor honor the person of the mighty: but in righteousness shalt thou judge thy neighbor.*

Did you catch it? These apostates were using flattery to get their way. They used flattery to maneuver their way into positions in the church, to get on the good side of those in authority.

Moses wrote in Leviticus you're not to honor anyone above another person, but to treat all with the same respect as a Christian should.

James dealt with this in chapter 2 verses 1-9. You're not to have respect for someone who may have money verses someone who doesn't. Also, you're not to have respect over someone who wears nicer things or drives nicer vehicles, etc.

Showing this type of respect isn't a godly trait and God doesn't approve of this type of behavior. So, Jude said in this verse; that these apostates were discontent, fulfilled their own wicked desires, used flattery on them to get their own way.

Have you ever seen this before in the local church? Or even in the workplace. As Christians, we need to be aware of the practices and traits of an apostate.

We need to be wise in spotting these types of people within the church, for they can destroy the local church. Today, we don't have to worry about the government taking over the church, nor the businesses, or the cults, but, those who call themselves Christians but, have no traits of a Christian.

These are who we need to look out for. We are to be on guard always, ready to defend our church and our church family.

Jude 17-But, beloved, remember ye the words which were spoken before of the apostles of our Lord Jesus Christ.

But, beloved- Now we come to Jude's address. Who was he speaking to? Who were the beloved? First, the word beloved means *dear to the heart, loved.* He was speaking to the readers, the early Christians of his day. And today, as you study this epistle, he is speaking to you. You are the beloved, the beloved of God.

So, even today he says **but, beloved…** and we answer him; Yes Jude, what is it?

Remember ye the words which were spoken before of the apostles of our Lord Jesus Christ- Now, Jude began to address the problem. Allow me to say this before we continue to what Jude wanted us to remember. The original readers of this epistle, did not have the completed New Testament in leather back, to keep and read at their leisure. No, it was harder for them. What they knew of the apostles were from mostly letters, mingled with Scripture references.

If they were lucky, they might have a page or partial page of a copy of an apostle's writing to pass around. It's sad to note that you and I have the complete word of God, and it stays out in our car, more than in our hands. It stays on the desk, or the book shelf, or the dresser, somewhere, anywhere but in our hands. Shame on us. Shame, we have it so easy in America, to purchase the word of God, and most of us have multiple copies of it, yet, we never take time to read it.

In America, we've lost the appreciation for it, some may not even know how many lives were sacrificed for you and me to hold a copy of His word in our hands. Allow me to read an excerpt from John Phillips book on Jude.

The great word is Remember!

But we cannot remember something that we have never known any more than we can remember someone whom we have never met. It is important, then, that we lay a good foundation in the Word. God expects us to know, study, and memorize His Word. He expects us to have a systematic theology, a consistent hermeneutics and a comprehensive grasp of revealed truth. Apostates trade on ignorance. - (Taken from Exploring the Epistle of Jude © Copyright 2004 by John Phillips. Published by Kregel Publications, Grand Rapids, MI. Used by permission of the publisher. All rights reserved.)

Why is it important that we remember these truths that the apostles wrote? So, we aren't duped into the lies of these apostates. You shall know the truth, and the truth shall make you what? free. Without truth, you will forever be in bondage.

Jude 18-**How that they told you there should be mockers in the last time who should walk after their own ungodly lust.**

This word <u>mockers</u>, that Jude used could also be *scoffers*. With that, I am reminded of those who scoffed at Christ. Caiaphas; the soldiers; the thief on the cross; and others. What did these do? They laughed at Him, they mocked and criticized Him.

Paul, in the book of Acts said it like this; Chapter 20:29-*For I know this, that after my departing shall grievous wolves enter in among you, not sparing the flock.* The phrase <u>grievous wolves</u>, means: *hurtful, destructive; causing mischief and a wolf is a beast of prey that kills sheep…. The wolf is crafty, greedy and eager for gratification.*

This is what a grievous wolf is. This is also exactly what an apostate is. Not only does the apostate want your position in the church, not only do they want to harm your family, but spiritually they want to kill you.

How do they do this? By hurting you so bad that you become bitter. You become hurt and upset to where you're no good to God for anything and you're no good to yourself either.

Apostates, like wolves, have an instinct to hurt, lame, and kill. Don't think that they will be satisfied with just having you out of the way. They won't stop until the entire church has split or shut its doors.

What did Paul say there at the end? *not sparing the flock.* I am also reminded of what Paul said to Timothy.

1 Timothy 4:1, 2- *Now the Spirit speaketh expressly, that in the latter times some shall depart from the faith, giving heed to seducing spirits, and doctrines of devils; Speaking lies in hypocrisy; having their conscience seared with a hot iron;*

Let us look at these two verses for a moment. Now we know that we are in the latter times. I've personally dealt with an apostate, he did all he could to bring about discord, strife, he attacked me, the preacher, and others. Why did he do this? How did he get that way? Did he just decide that he would become an apostate one day? It never happens that way. Paul said, they depart from the faith.

Why? Because they gave in to these seducing spirits, and doctrines of devils. The flesh, the world, or someone came along and filled their head full of garbage.

Then in the second verse we see where Paul said, having their conscience seared with a hot iron. This term means that they can't feel conviction anymore. They are numbed to any sense of the Holy Spirit's touch. I don't know for sure, but I would guess that they are past the stage of salvation, they have totally rejected God. I hope that I'm wrong.

Then lastly for this verse in Jude, let us look at one other thing that Paul has written down over in the next book. 2 Timothy 3:1-5 *This know also, that in the last days perilous times shall come. For men shall be lovers of their own selves, covetous, boasters, proud, blasphemers, disobedient to parents, unthankful, unholy, without natural affection, truce breakers, false accusers, incontinent, fierce, despisers of those that are good, traitors, heady, high minded, lovers of pleasures more than lovers of God; having a form of godliness, but denying the power thereof: from such turn away.*

I don't want to get too detailed in dissecting these verses but I do want to go over a few things with you.

Paul said again that in the last days perilous times shall come. Someone might have asked, "what's going to happen Paul?" He then listed several key things that you and I can see going on in this world today. Not only in the world, but more shamefully within the local church.

Paul stated the following;

1. Men shall be lovers of their own selves, and not of God or their neighbors.

2. Covetous-they become lovers of money, doing the basest of things to obtain it.

3. Boasters-of what they have, or are, or can do.

4. Proud-thinking highly of themselves on these accounts.

5. Blasphemers-of God, and revilers of their fellow-creatures.

6. Disobedient to parents-not withstanding all the obligations they are under their authority.

7. Unthankful- to other benefactors, and to God for the blessings of providence and grace.

8. Unholy- though they profess themselves to be devoted to God, and consecrated to his service by the most solemn rites.

9. Without natural affection- even to their own children, as well as of piety toward their parents.

10. Truce breakers-those who are unwilling to enter into any agreement; not willing to reconcile to others when there is a variance.

11. False accusers-they don't mind slandering others.

12. Incontinent- Not restraining the passions or appetites, particularly the sexual appetite, indulging in lust without restraint.

13. Fierce-meaning cruel in their revenge.

14. Despisers of those that are good-if you are a Christian and right with God, look out, you will be despised.

15. Traitors-they would give up their own brethren into the hands of persecutors, and those who oppose their corrupt practices, to death.

16. Heady-rash in enterprising things which can only issue in the disturbance of society, or the ruin of those that undertake them.

17. High minded-puffed up with such insolence and self-sufficiency as to dispose any remonstrance which can be made to bring them to a wiser and more decent conduct.

18. Lovers of pleasures more than lovers of God-namely sensual pleasure, and who will therefore sacrifice all considerations of religion to the gratification of their appetites.

19. Having a form of godliness- in observing with exactness the rituals and external ordinances of religion, but not regarding, nay even denying and blaspheming the inward power and reality of it.

Paul concluded at the end of verse five, *from such turn away*. Don't get involved with these types of people. They will only cause hurt, shame, and destruction upon your family.

These are the mockers Jude spoke of in this verse. Today, they continue to **walk after their own ungodly lust.**

Jude 19-**These be they who separate themselves, sensual, having not the Spirit.**

These be they who separate themselves- This reminds me of what Solomon spoke of in Proverbs 18:1-*Through desire a man, having separated himself, seeketh and intermeddleth with all wisdom.* But I don't think that is what Jude was speaking about when he said this.

These apostates were not separating themselves to seek wisdom, nor to draw closer to God. Nay, they were separating themselves to draw closer to their own lusts. For the fulfillment of their own lusts.

We are told in Romans 16:17- *Now I beseech you, brethren, mark them which cause divisions and offenses contrary to the doctrine which ye have learned; and avoid them.*

That's fine that they have separated themselves from us considering their religion. He was speaking of false religions, cults. Those religions that say they are Christians, but deny the Savior and say that you must add to what Christ did for us in order to be saved.

If any religion or church says that you must work for salvation, then they are wrong. Salvation is by grace through faith. Faith in the finished work of our Lord Jesus Christ.

I wished that he was saying that they were separating themselves unto God as Solomon says for Christians to do, but they are not. What did Jude continue to say in this verse?

Sensual, having not the Spirit- We've just looked at that word sensual. Paul spoke of it in 2 Timothy. Here in the book of Jude, this word sensual means, *unregenerate.* Anyone who is not saved. So, the acid test is, do they have the spirit in them?

Jude ended the verse stating; **having not the Spirit.** We must remember that we are not dealing with Christians when dealing with apostates. They are brute beasts, they are animals. They are the basest of men and women.

There is not a limit to what they will do for their own gratification. This is why you have pastors marrying same sex couples. This is why you have pastors saying that it's ok to abort unborn children, not fetuses, but children! This is why you have pastors that are actively having sexual affairs with members of their church. This is why you have pastors that commit the most heinous crimes of nature, because they are apostates and not Christians!

Don't underestimate the wickedness that a man can do. You and I as Christians need to stand guard over the church, over our families, even over our own selves. Don't get lazy, don't give up, don't think that it's someone else's job and that you don't have to do it. Once you get relaxed, you become the target.

Keep your morals high, keep your faith strong, and keep your eyes on Jesus! Don't ever give up, don't ever give in, and don't ever compromise with the devil. You can't afford to do that.

Jude 20-But Ye, beloved, building up yourselves on your most holy faith, praying in the Holy Ghost.

After constantly giving them examples of what to look out for, and illustrations of what apostates look and act like, Jude then brought his readers into the picture. He will now venture out giving them a threefold command. We see this in verses twenty and twenty-one. They are to Build, pray and look. As we dissect these verses we will look at each of these and learn how we can obey God in practicing these commands.

But ye- He said now I want to give you some instruction. Today, let's listen to Jude. Put aside the differences of denominations and the differences of culture, and lets you and I listen to Jude. For he wasn't speaking to a denomination or a culture, but to Christians. Often, we get wrapped up in so many minor subdivisions of mankind, that we forget that God sees us as lost or redeemed. It would do us good to look at others the way God sees us.

Beloved- We've spoke about this word before when Jude used it in verse three. The Greek word is Agapitos. This word means *divinely loved ones-* Wuest. So, when was the last time you remembered that you are beloved? Beloved of God, beloved of Christ, so much in that He came to this earth to live, and to die so that we may spend eternity with Him. How's that for beloved?

Building up yourselves- The first of the three commands given by Jude in this verse. The term building up means *resting on your most holy faith as a foundation, making progress, rise like an edifice higher and higher. To edify.* So, Jude said, or God rather commanded us through Jude, to build ourselves. We are to appropriately build on, following a plan with pre-designed specifications, that God has already given us. That's the Christian life, that's the godly way.

Ok, so we are commanded to build or be building up ourselves. How do we do so? Over in I Corinthians 10:23 Paul said-*All things are lawful for me, but all things are not expedient:* expedient meaning *useful or profitable. All things are lawful for me, but all things edify not.*

To some, you may know that Paul was speaking of the question of the eating of meat offered to idols. In Paul's explanation, he directly stated an important principle of Christian Liberty; *"all things are lawful for me."* But we must remember, what effect does our action have upon our self and what effect does it have on others?

96

Don't get me wrong, I love the liberty we have received through Christ, but we mustn't allow our liberty to cause ourselves nor others to stumble in the faith.

Moving on, though something we might do may be lawful for us, however, it may not be proper. In view of this, Jude said what? **building up yourselves**. How do we build up ourselves? How do we edify ourselves? Well, it's in our everyday lifestyle, how we dress, what we spend our money on, our entertainment, and how we interact with this world that we live in.

Paul then moved to the mode of worship. In 1Corinthians 14:26-*How is it then, brethren, when ye come together, every one of you hath a psalm, hath a doctrine, hath a tongue, hath a revelation, hath an interpretation. Let all things be done unto edifying.*

Did you catch that last phrase? *"Let all things be done unto edifying."* Everything in the church. Not just the preaching, not just the singing, but everything. In God's house, we are to be in a constant edifying mode. If a church has a great spirit about it, it's because the congregation is actively involved in edifying. They aren't worried if they weren't picked for the upcoming special. They aren't worried if they were told they're not needed in the nursery. Why? Because everything they do is unto edifying.

The moment we lose sight of this important principle in our lives, in our churches, then we will lose the joy of God's peace. Paul went on to say in 1 Corinthians 14:33-*For God is not the author of confusion, but of peace, as in all churches of the saints.* When a church ceases to have the peace of God upon them, when you and I cease to have God's peace upon our own lives, then somewhere we've gotten away from edifying.

Look at Ephesians 4:29-*Let no corrupt communication proceed out of your mouth, but that which is good to the use of edifying, that it may minister grace unto the hearers.* How do we continue building up ourselves? Paul gave us a twofold answer;

First, we are to make sure that we have no corrupt communication proceeding out of our mouths. That word corrupt is sapros in the Greek and means *rotten or worthless*. So, our communication and thoughts that are turned into words, are not to be rotten words, morally speaking. They are not to be worthless words, vain or unproductive.

Have you ever known someone to talk too much? Well, most likely they are speaking corrupt words, worthless, vain words. Ever known a hot head? Most likely you've heard them speak rotten, harmful derogative words. As a Christian, we know better. But how often do we slip with our tongues, words that are corrupt. How often do we sadden or even repulse our Lord with our corrupt words?

Remember what James said about our tongue? In James 3:5, 6 and 8-10- *Even so the tongue is a little member, and boasteth great things. Behold, how great a matter a little fire kindleth! And the tongue is a fire, a world of iniquity: so is the tongue among our members, that it defileth the whole body, and setteth on fire the course of nature; and it is set on fire of hell. But the tongue can no man tame; it is an unruly evil, full of deadly poison. Therewith bless we God, even the Father; and therewith curse we men, which are made after the similitude of God. Out of the same mouth proceedeth blessing and cursing. My brethren, these things ought not so to be.*

Do you see how he ended verse 10? My friend, he is speaking to us. He then said, *"these things ought not so to be."* What things was he talking about? Did you see what James said in verse five? Our tongue, though small gets Christians into more trouble than any other part of our body. Why is that? Because we haven't yet figured out how to conquer it.

Day after day we allow our words to hurt, degrade, scoff at, complain, humiliate, and sometimes cuss. We don't only do this at the world, no, we say these things to our own loved ones. To our families, our brethren inside the church. Shame on us for this type of behavior.

Let's look at Colossians 2:6,7-*As ye have therefore received Christ Jesus the Lord, so walk ye in him: Rooted and built up in him, and stablished in the faith, as ye have been taught, abounding therein with thanksgiving.*

What does that mean? To walk in him? Paul was saying that we have Christ as our example of what we are to say, what we are to do, where we are to go, how we are to live. He is our standard of living. Our life should be patterned after his life. His standards, convictions, morals, etc. should be reflected in our lives.

The term <u>rooted</u> means *to cause a person to be thoroughly grounded.* Here's that phrase built up again. This has the same meaning as Jude spoke of. *To edify, following a plan with pre-designed specifications.* What was Paul saying then?

Elliott says:

Paul bids them seek not only the first basis of their faith, both their continual growth, in Christ alone, by continual "strengthening in the faith" which rests in Him.

So Jude was saying to always be "building up" edifying ourselves and each other, in the faith. We are to watch out for those things that do not edify, though we might have the liberty to do those things, it's often gonna cause someone, quite possibly yourself, to stumble.

Then within the church we are to do all things for edification. Knowing that it is better to be wronged, than to wrong someone else. There are to be no schisms within the body of believers. Next, we are to watch what we say. Our tongue is to edify not to pull down our fellow believers. Noting what James said about the tongue, we are to keep it under subjection always.

Then lastly concerning edifying, we are to ever continue to grow in our faith in Christ Jesus our Lord. Salvation is only the beginning. We have a Christian walk to work at daily. Though many days we might fail, we are to get back up and go on for Christ, our Supreme example.

On your most holy faith- Ok, so Jude was saying that we need to always be edifying ourselves on or with our most holy faith. Then where does this faith come from? How do we use or build ourselves upon our faith?

First, let us look at where we obtain faith. Look at Romans 10:17-*So then faith cometh by hearing, and hearing by the word of God.* This tells me that to believe the Word, the Word must be spoken. The unregenerate will not think to themselves, "hey, I've never heard about this Jesus, but I think that I'll go ahead and trust Him as my Savior." No, that doesn't happen.

How can a person trust in something or someone they've never heard of? To have faith you must have something to put your faith in. That's where the Word of God comes in. Then once we receive faith, faith in Christ, then we build upon that faith.

It says over in 1 John 5:4-*For whatsoever is born of God overcometh the world: and this is the victory that overcometh the world, even our faith.* How do we overcome the world? By our faith. Our faith, when received by us, also allows us to receive the Holy Spirit. To which allows us to be able to build up ourselves on our most holy faith. Without the Spirit, it would be impossible for us to ever overcome any spiritual obstacles we face.

Look at what else Jude said in this verse, we'll finish it right here.

Praying in the Holy Ghost- This is the second command given by Jude to his readers, along with us today. How well does this command dovetail into his first command of edifying? What better way for us to build up than in the spirit of prayer?

Look with me at Romans 8:26-*Likewise the Spirit also helpeth our infirmities: for we know not what we should pray for as we ought: but the Spirit itself make the intercession for us with groanings which cannot be uttered.*

I am reminded of how you and I need the unhindered presence of the Holy Spirit in our prayers. Why is that? Paul said in the above text, the Spirit also helpeth our infirmities; that word <u>infirmity</u> refers to *an ailment that deprives someone of enjoying or accomplishing what they would like to do.* So, the Spirit provides the necessary ability for us to be heard by God. Why? Paul went on to say, for we know not what we should pray for as we ought. So, we need the Holy Spirit's companionship.

Of course, Paul gave us a myriad of examples in his epistles. Let's look at Galatians 4:6-*And because ye are sons, God hath sent forth the Spirit of his Son into your hearts, crying, Abba, Father.* What does it advantage us to have the (Spirit of his Son in our hearts?)

Jude commanded us to pray in the Holy Ghost, which is something that only a Christian can do. Therefore, by having that ability, we know that we have been bought, we are now adopted children of God. The Creator is not some distant higher power to be feared, but we have a relationship with the Creator. Not so much as Creator/creation but a closer bond. A cord, the Creator is now known as our Father, while we are now known as His children.

That is why the Holy Spirit is heard crying Abba, Father from our hearts to God Almighty. This is the token of the never-ending bond that we now have with the Father.

So, when Jude commanded to pray in the Holy Ghost, it's not some hard-trifling task, but a natural ability of asking, as you would ask of your own earthly parents of a need or help. The Spirit brings your needs to God while God through the Spirit answers those needs. What an awesome communion we have with God through the Holy Spirit.

So, we looked at two of Jude's commands in this verse. We've seen how Jude is beckoning us to edify, for our own personal walk and for our talk. Constantly be on the lookout for how we treat others, what we say, and being God conscious in our lives.

Then Jude said to do so on our most holy faith. Our foundation is laid by faith, and we continue to build upon that faith all our lives. Then lastly, praying in the Spirit. Christians have a unique relationship with the Creator of this world. One that we can know as our God, for we know Him as Father.

Today, where are you at in your Christian walk? Have you forgotten that God is your Heavenly Father? Have you forgotten that we need to be building up others? Also, we ourselves need to be in prayer with God? This is a constant duty we have.

Jude 21-**Keep yourselves in the love of God, looking for the mercy of our Lord Jesus Christ unto eternal life.**

Keep yourselves- The word <u>keep</u> means *to watch over; to guard.* I think that to explain this part of the verse, a verse that Paul wrote would help us out. Let's look over in Acts 11:23-*Who, when he came, and had seen the grace of God, was glad, and exhorted them all, that with purpose of heart they would cleave unto the Lord.*

I want us to look at this word <u>cleave.</u> It means; *to remain attached to; abide in.* Paul told us to abide in the Lord. This is a constant abiding. But it goes so much deeper than this constant abiding.

The phrase <u>with purpose</u> means; *to be resolute or having a fixed purpose; determined; constant in pursuing a purpose.* Did you catch that? We are to be resolute or determined in our hearts to cleave unto the Lord.

We are to be men and women with determination that we won't stop until we accomplish the act of abiding. So, Jude said for us to "**keep yourselves.**"

What exactly did he mean by this? We are to (with resolute determination) watch over and guard ourselves. The military would use a phrase such as, "at all costs!"

Ok then, guard ourselves, keep ourselves at what or from what?

In the love of God- Jude said to keep ourselves, to guard ourselves not from something but in something, **in the love of God.** We are to keep ourselves in the love of God.

Why is it so important to keep yourselves, "in the love of God?" Why does he think that it's so important that he had to tell us this after all the illustrations and cautions that he wrote to us about apostasy?

At this period in my life, I would say that it's not hard to realize the importance. I've dealt with an apostate first hand, and let me say that it was all that I could do not to get bitter.

Let's see if we can look into the Bible to explain what Jude meant by keeping yourselves in the love of God.

Paul said in Romans 5:5-*And hope maketh not ashamed; because the love of God is shed abroad in our hearts by the Holy Ghost which is given unto us.* That phrase <u>shed abroad</u> means *poured out.*

So, if I'm reading this correctly, the love of our God has been poured out into our hearts.

The Holy Spirit gives our souls a rich sense of the greatness of God's love for us. (Thayer's Greek Lexicon.)

And get this, we received this love of God at the same time of our salvation, upon the receiving of the Holy Spirit. I am reminded of 1 John 4:7,8- **Beloved, let us love one another: for love is of God; and every one that loveth is born of God, and knoweth God. He that loveth not knoweth not God; for God is love.**

Let me say this, if you fill a bottle with water and it spills over, what will come out? Water. Ok, if we are fill to the capacity with the love of God, and we get spiritually tipped over, what should come out? Correct, the love of God.

How come most church goers today, when they are 'tipped over' all you see is hate, anger, violence. Why is that? Because they have either grieved the Holy Spirit or they have never received the Holy Spirit. One or the other, I suspect that it is the latter.

Jude said to keep ourselves in the love of God. How do we perform that impossible task? Is it impossible? Can Christians keep themselves in the love of God? Meaning continually?

Well, we've just seen where Paul said that Christians have the indwelling Holy Spirit in them, which has shed or poured the love of God upon their hearts.

Paul continued to give an example in the book of Romans 8:37-39- **Nay, in all these things we are more than conquerors through him that loved us. For I am persuaded, that neither death, nor life, nor angels, nor principalities, nor powers, nor things present, nor things to come, nor height, nor depth, nor any other creature, shall be able to separate us from the love of God, which is in Christ Jesus our Lord.**

Back up to verse 35-**Who shall separate us from the love of Christ?** Paul asked a unique question here. Then in the same verse he listed several examples of what one might believe would or could separate them from God's love. But, in reality, nothing can separate us from the love of God.

Once we are saved, we have the Holy Spirit dwelling within us. That Holy Spirit is the supplier of God's love, the fountain to which it flows to our hearts. Now, nothing we can do will ever take the Holy Spirit away from us.

Though we may hinder the Spirit, He is forever with us. So, Paul was right in saying that we are more than conquerors. Not of our own self but through him that loved us, though Christ Jesus our Lord.

So, we don't have to work at keeping the love of God in us. We only work at allowing the love of God to flow out of our lives. Toward our neighbors, toward our families, toward our coworkers, and church families.

We can never be separated from the Holy Spirit, nor the love that He sheds on our hearts, but we can hinder the job of the Holy Spirit by allowing sin to take hold of our lives. That would cause our outward flow of God's love to congeal but never the inward flow of His love upon our hearts.

Besides, Paul also said in 2 Thessalonians 3:5-*And the Lord direct your hearts into the love of God, and into the patient waiting for Christ.* The Lord is in control, you will receive the love of God, if you are a Christian.

Looking for- That term looking for means *expecting.* I am reminded of a pregnant woman and what they are often referred to as, and that's expecting.

Why is it that a woman pregnant is spoken of in that way? What is she expecting? She is looking for, or expecting that, out of the pain of the pregnancy, the months of gaining weight, the changes in her body and the pain of child birth, that she will one day be rewarded with a child.

Not just any child, but her child. So, she willingly waits those long months, overweight, in constant pain, with swelling legs and hands. She goes through the three to twenty-four hours of relentless child birth, knowing that the cost was very much worth it. So, she goes on; how? Simply expecting. Expecting that one day the reward will come and she can forget the nine months of agony.

I am reminded of Paul's words to Titus, in chapter 2:13-*Looking for that blessed hope, and the glorious appearing of the great God and our Saviour Jesus Christ.* Paul told Titus, hey, we are to be looking for that blessed hope, the return of our Lord. So, what was Titus to do? He was to be expecting. Expecting the return of our Savior.

Yes, you and I will have trials here on this earth. We will go through pain and heartache. We will suffer and become familiar with loss. But, we should be expecting a better day ahead. Not on this earth, but in heaven. Expect that one day, our nine months of bearing our pains and labor will be rewarded with a new life without any heartaches, without any loss, except for our sin nature.

Jude said to be looking for, or expecting. Expecting what?

The mercy of our Lord Jesus Christ- Mercy means *pity or compassion.* Strong's says of this word for this verse; *the mercy of Christ, whereby at his return to judgment he will bless true Christians with eternal life:*

Paul said in Titus 3:5-*Not by works of righteousness which we have done, but according to his mercy he saved us, by the washing of regeneration, and renewing of the Holy Ghost;*

We must always remember that the mercy of God is a gift, not a bill of right. Too often you and I forget that as Isaiah said in 64:6-*But we are all as an unclean thing, and all our righteousnesses are as filthy rags; and we all do fade as a leaf; and our iniquities, like the wind have taken us away.*

Paul said, not by works of righteousness which we have done. Why not Paul? Because Isaiah said all our righteousness are as filthy rags. Who are we to deserve mercy? Who are we to look at God and say "that's my mercy you have, now give it to me!"

Day in and day out we abuse the mercy of God. We keep believing that it's ours, and that we deserve it. No! Not one bit. What we deserve is an eternity in the pits of hell.

Isaiah said that we are as an unclean thing. But despite this truth, Paul stated that per His mercy, not my good works or my righteousness, but per His mercy He saved us.

The moment you understand that you are worthless, apart from the blood of Christ shed for you, you will then become useful for the ministry. Only then. We have no talents but what is provided by God. We have no righteousness apart from what God provides.

So, this mercy of the Lord Jesus Christ, where will it take us? Jude finished this verse by saying;

Unto eternal life- This is a wonderful statement. Jude reminded us that our Christian life isn't over once we die, but that our life will be forever in heaven because Christ gave us eternal life.

It's through His mercy that we will be remembered when we die and taken to heaven. This is the capstone of the gift that Christ purchased for us when He died on Calvary.

Paul said in Romans 6:23-*For the wages of sin is death; but the gift of God is eternal life through Jesus Christ our Lord.* All throughout our lives we've been earning a wage. The older we get the more of a wage we've accumulated. Then once we pass from this life to the next, we must cash out our wages.

Those who have rejected Christ and His gift, will have their payment in full, forever in total darkness and torment day and night, away from the mercy and grace of our Lord. Those of us who have received the precious gift of God, the payment of our sin was applied to Christ on the cross. We will never see those wages. Not of any righteousness that we have apart from Christ's righteousness.

Paul explained this righteousness of Christ in Romans 5:21-*That as sin hath reigned unto death, even so might grace reign through righteousness unto eternal life by Jesus Christ our Lord.*

Death has always been brought about because of sin. But because of the love of our Savior, Christ's grace reign through righteousness, meaning His righteousness, unto eternal life, and that grace is by none other than Jesus Christ our Lord.

Our salvation, is a precious gift, that shouldn't be taken lightly. The eternal Son of God paid the ultimate sacrifice for it and we should keep that in mind daily.

So, Jude told us in this verse to guard ourselves, in the precious love of God that the Holy Spirit provides for us. We are to be expecting that through God's mercy He will bring us into eternal life.

What a wonderful thought for you and me today. Why don't you take a moment and just thank God for His wonderful salvation?

Jude 22-**And of some have compassion, making a difference:**

I know several people that have this verse for their life verse or maybe as a favorite verse. I want us to look at it a little closer before we move on to the next one.

The word compassion means *to bring help to those who are very miserable; those who have sunk into deep affliction or distress, either from want, anxiety or grief.* That last phrase "making a difference" means *those who separate themselves from you, that have apostatized.*

So, we are to have compassion on those that have left their faith either due to their affliction, due to greed. It could also have been by trickery that they left their faith, and now we are to show them compassion. In doing so we are making a difference.

Paul said in Galatians 6:1-***Brethren, if a man be overtaken in a fault, ye which are spiritual, restore such an one in the spirit of meekness; considering thyself, lest thou also be tempted.***

In this verse the word overtaken means *to be caught, overtaken or taken by surprise.* Basically, your caught before you have the chance to flee from the act of sin or before you can conceal your sin, your crime.

Then the word spiritual means *one who is filled with and governed by the Holy Spirit.* This is a must for anyone who plans on helping a fallen brother in Christ. What right do we have as Christians to help restore another child of God when we ourselves need to be restored.

Basically, Paul knew what you and I know today, and that is, if you're not right with God, then you're not going to be making wise decisions. You will probably be more judgmental and callus towards that person and do more harm than good.

How dare we become Judge and jury of our fallen brethren. Where's the helping hand when it's needed? You and I have a duty to keep ourselves spiritual, so that we may be a help to others that are needing help. Who else do they have to turn to?

Paul said ***in the spirit of meekness.*** That word meekness is a powerful word. It means *For the believer, meekness begins with the Lord's inspiration and finishes by His direction and empowerment. It is a divinely-balanced virtue that can only operate through faith.* (HELPS Word-studies)

We are not to confuse this powerful word 'meekness' with the word 'weakness.' For meekness is born of inner strength that is reserved, and it is sprinkled out from one with holy reserve. Our greatest Old Testament example of meekness was Moses, but our all-time best example is and will always be Christ our Lord.

This meekness is used while we help to restore our fallen brethren. We nurse and guide them back to the fold, as a shepherd does a wondering sheep. All the while we remind ourselves that it's only by the grace of our Lord that we aren't in the same situation. That's why Paul said *"considering yourself."* We are human, and we are bent towards sin. It's a constant struggle for all of us to live for God. Now I want us to look for a moment at what James said.

We see in James chapter 5:19,20-*Brethren, if any of you do err from the truth, and one convert him; Let him know, that he which converteth the sinner from the error of his way shall save a soul from death, and shall hide a multitude of sins.*

We see right off the bat, that James was speaking to Christians. He said *"brethren."* He said that if one of us err from the gospel truth, and it can happen, it does happen. Today, we shouldn't be so quick to judge our fallen brethren, but rather, lend our hand to them and help them up. Most Christians today, the ones that err, never come back to the sheep fold on one account. It's not that Christ isn't willing to accept them back, it's you and I that aren't willing.

That's right. Our self-righteousness separates us and the fallen. We make it impossible for them to come back, because we want them to come crawling, carrying the full weight of their sin upon their shoulders. When all God wants from them is to repent, to turn back. See that's what that word convert James uses means *to cause to return, or to bring back.*

All God wants is for His prodigal son to back come home. Why can't we realize this important truth? Jude said "**and of some have compassion, making a difference.**" Do you have compassion? Will you make a difference?

Jude 23-**And others save with fear, pulling them out of the fire; hating even the garment spotted by the flesh.**

And others save with fear- Now here is a second group of wayward Christians. These are more stubborn than your average. It could be that they've been convinced by the apostates into believing the lies of Satan. We have a more serious work on our hands as fellow believers in helping these persons. Paul gave us several examples of how to handle the stubborn Christian in need of repentance.

1 Corinthians 5:3-5- *For I verily, as absent in the body, but present in the spirit, have judged already, as though I were present, concerning him that hath so done this deed, in the name of our Lord Jesus Christ, when ye are gathered together, and my spirit, with the power of our Lord Jesus Christ, to deliver such an one unto Satan for the destruction of the flesh, that the spirit may be saved in the day of the Lord Jesus.*

In these verses, Paul was dealing with fornication within the church. A young man was sleeping with his father's new wife. Sadly, the church did nothing about it, but, instead they were *"puffed up"* Paul said. Now, in these verses, Paul laid out the church discipline that they were to follow.

He said, *"deliver such an one unto Satan for the destruction of the flesh."* Now Paul wasn't saying that this person was to lose their salvation. He was indicating that this person was not displaying any Christian attributes.

This person was living like the world therefore he should be treated like an unregenerate person. Was he saved? Yes. And therefore, even more, that is why the church needed to discipline this individual.

The church should never condone open sin. Once this has happened we cause the church to be susceptible to the chastisement of God. But as always if the church stands firm on correct discipline, then you be will more likely to have a strong godly church.

Paul gave us this instruction, not to shame anyone, but as he stated; *"that the spirit may be saved in the day of the Lord Jesus."* Paul wasn't concerned about the temporal, but the eternal. He knew that if this wasn't dealt with here and now than it would have to be dealt with once they stood before the Lord. You and I are better off, dealing with our sin here and now.

Paul then explained over in 2 Corinthians 7:10-12-*For godly sorrow worketh repentance to salvation not to be repented of: but the sorrow of the world worketh death. For behold this selfsame thing, that ye sorrowed after a godly sort, what carefulness it wrought in you, yea, what clearing of yourselves, yea, what indignation, yea, what fear, yea, what vehement desire, yea, what zeal, yea, what revenge! In all things ye have approved yourselves to be clear in this matter. Wherefore, though I wrote unto you, I did it not for his cause that had done the wrong, nor for his cause that suffered wrong, but that our care for you in the sight of God might appear unto you.*

What's going on here? Paul was speaking in this second letter to the Corinthians about this same person that took his father's wife. He said at the end of these verses; *"I did it not for his cause that had done the wrong, nor for his cause that suffered wrong, but that our care for you in the sight of God might appear unto you."*

He said, though the discipline was handed out to the person in the wrong, it wasn't all together for him only, nor for the father that suffered the wrong. But, more importantly it was for the body of believers. Look at the list of benefits listed in verse eleven:

1. They had godly sorrow. Instead of being "puffed up" about the open sin, they became sorrowful, knowing that this sin was causing the church body to "stink" in the sight of the community.
2. They became <u>careful</u>. This word here means *that they became earnest in doing God's will once they knew His will.* So, when Paul scolded them in the first letter, they learned the will of God and therefore sought to accomplish His will.
3. They cleared their name. The word <u>clearing</u> used here is in the aspect of *a Christian defending their faith.* They cleared their name by giving a good defense on the terms they stood on.
4. They had indignation. They were wroth, or angry against the sin that was shaming the church and hindering the gospel from spreading.
5. They feared. This is the good kind of fear that every church member should have. They feared that if they didn't completely amputate the affected area then the disease of sin could spread once again.
6. They had vehement desire. I think this desire was towards accomplishing the will of God.
7. They had zeal. This zeal was their emotions hot with the desire to please Paul, whom they loved.

8. Lastly, they had revenge. This speaks of the punishment that was laid out to the offender. Paul told them *'to deliver such an one unto Satan for the destruction of the flesh.'* This punishment was equal to the offense which was delivered to the church.

Pulling them out of the fire- Jude said that some can't be spared with compassion, nor fear, but they must be "pulled" from their own destruction, out of the fire. Sin, like any drug, is addictive. Once it has its death grips attached to you, you need help pulling away from them.

Jude knew all too well the importance of proactive restoration. A Christian who is knee deep in sin, can't think straight, nor do they know how to make the right decisions for themselves. That's why we as brethren, reach out, with compassion, with fear, but also with urgency as if one was about to be consumed by fire. This isn't a physical pull on them, but a desperate pull at their heart.

Let's look at what Paul had to say about it, 2 Corinthians 5:10,11-*For we must all appear before the judgment seat of Christ; that every one may receive the things done in his body, according to that he hath done, whether it be good or bad. Knowing therefore the terror of the Lord, we persuade men; but we are made manifest unto God; and I trust also are made manifest in your consciences.*

That phrase 'but we are made manifest unto God' means *that we are to become known, thoroughly understood.* Paul said that every one of us will give an account to God. That we should keep in the forefront of our minds the terror of God and know that God knows what we do, we can't hide anything from Him.

We are to urge those, who have left their love for Christ, and pull at their hearts to make them understand what they are doing is wrong, that they can't hide their wicked lifestyle from the Creator. We are to show the urgency in our actions, but also our own lifestyle should reflect our sincere Christian attitude. Our pull upon them will be stronger when we ourselves are closer to our Lord.

Hating even the garment spotted by the flesh- What a picture that is painted here by Jude. This is a very descriptive sentence, but allow me to be as discrete as possible.

Jude was giving us an example of how dirty we can become if we walk out on God and follow our lustful desires. He was reminding us of how God views sin. In hopes of you and I viewing it the exact same way so as not to defile ourselves by the same perversion as the apostates.

This phrase 'garment spotted by the flesh' means *such as an undergarment that bodily fluids have been excreted on.* You and I would be repulsed by such a polluted picture, and so is God by those who live such a wicked lifestyle.

So, in these two verses, Jude told us that we need to go after those that wander away from the Lord. We see that compassion can bring some in, though others are brought back with fear. Then lastly, he said that if they are so far gone, then we need to plead with them to come back. But, we do it in fear of what they are doing, lest we ourselves get caught up in their sins.

Jude 24-**Now unto him that is able to keep you from falling, and to present you faultless before the presence of his glory with exceeding joy,**

We are now going to be looking at Jude's closing statements. We have covered so much in these few verses. Jude then prepared his goodbye, and reminded them of the ultimate power of God. Let's look at this.

Now unto him that is able to keep you from falling- I am quickly reminded of the doxology given by the apostle Paul at the end of his magnum opus, the epistle to the Romans. In chapter 16:25 Paul said, *"Now to him that is of power to stablish you according to my gospel...."*

What a worthy praise to give the God of our salvation. Let's go over some noteworthy reminders of why we should praise him. For He is worthy of our praise.

Jude said that God is able. How do we know this? The book of John records for us in chapter 10:29,30-*My Father, which gave them me, is greater than all; and no man is able to pluck them out of my Father's hand. I and my Father are one.* These are the recorded words of Christ speaking to the Jews while he stood on Solomon's porch at the temple. A question arises, *"How long dost thou make us to doubt? If thou be the Christ, tell us plainly."*

We've just read his answer. What a marvelous statement; *"I and my Father are one."* There are times when we may doubt and say "can God?" Well Jude has answered that question, Yes! He is able! God can! How do we know this? Because Christ said that nobody can take you or me out of the Father's hand, and that He and the Father are one. We cannot be harmed without the Father allowing it to happen.

Do you realize that it's not a question of I hope that God can do it, it's a question of do I believe that He can do it? Because we serve a God who can! I'm reminded of what Paul said in Romans 8:31-*What shall we say then to these things? If God for us, who can be against us?*

In this life, who do we have to worry about? If you're in the will of God, who is it that your worried about? The answer should be no one.

In Ephesians 3:20-*Now unto him that is able to do exceeding abundantly above all that we ask or think, according to the power that worketh in us.* Paul said that we can't even comprehend the possibilities of what God can do for us. His power is beyond our imagination, beyond our expectations. We are talking about the Creator, not some formed being.

Then Paul said in 2 Timothy 4:18-*And the Lord shall deliver me from every evil work, and will preserve me unto his heavenly kingdom: to whom be glory for ever and ever. Amen.* He told Timothy, hey, God can preserve me, God is able to get me from here to my eternal home. God deserves the glory, from now till forever after. This is our God. The one Jude spoke of saying *"Now unto him that is able!"* Why?

Because Jude lived with the Son of God. Jude saw the resurrected Son of God, and he knew that if anyone could keep a promise, that it would be his older half-brother, Christ our Lord.

And to present you- That word <u>present</u> means *to cause one to make his appearance faultless before God.* What is the importance of bringing us before God the Father faultless? Why is it that Jude reminded his readers and us that Christ will 'present' us?

Paul said in 2 Corinthians 11:2-*For I am jealous over you with godly jealousy: for I have espoused you to one husband, that I may present you as a chaste virgin to Christ.* Paul's concern for the Corinthian church was that they would be corrupted by false teachers. So, his jealousy was for a good cause. He witnessed to them, they came to Christ, so then he fought to keep them separated unto God. Why?

He said that they as part of the church body, was to be kept clean, so that the bride of Christ, which is the church, could one day be presented to Christ as a <u>chaste virgin</u> meaning *pure and clean, free from defilement.*

Jude still reminds us of the importance of being a pure Christian. If the church is the bride of Christ, why shouldn't He have a pure bride? Why should He have anything less?

In Ephesians 5:27-*That he might present it to himself a glorious church, not having spot, or wrinkle, or any such thing; but that it should be holy and with out blemish.* Christ shouldn't have to settle for mediocrity. No, we should live our lives pleasing to Him so that once we are called up, we are presented to Him as Paul said, *"not having spot, or wrinkle, or any such thing; but that it should be holy and with out blemish."*

The word <u>spot</u> means *immoral stain upon the soul.* And <u>wrinkle</u> means, *a flaw, spiritual defect.* How many of us are showing wrinkles or spots upon our lives? How many of us have spiritual stains, that we allow to show up on our hearts?

When will we take our filth, and ask Christ to cleanse it? Don't you deserve better than to live like the world? We are Christians, we know better, we should do better. We have the Holy Spirit living within us, we have all the help we need. All you need is the desire to do so. How will He present us? Jude said;

Faultless- <u>Faultless</u> means *unblemished from the marring effects of sin.* What a glorious day that will be when we meet our blessed Lord, and he presents us faultless. No more sin nature. No more shame or fear. Only joy. What a day that will be.

Before the presence of his glory- There is coming a day when we shall be in the presence of the Most High. Paul put it like this in 1 Thessalonians 4:16,17-*For the Lord himself shall descend from heaven with a shout, with the voice of the archangel, and with the trump of God: and the dead in Christ shall rise first: Then we which are alive and remain shall be caught up together with them in the clouds, to meet the Lord in the air: and so, shall we ever be with the Lord.*

What a wonderful reminder of the coming of our Lord. Now this isn't speaking of the Second Coming, but of the rapture, when Christ shall come in the clouds. And while not ever touching down to earth, He will call His bride, the church up to meet Him in the air.

If that doesn't make you home sick, then I don't know what will. Jude then ended this verse with these words,

With exceeding joy- Peter said in 1 Peter 4:13-*But rejoice, in as much as ye are partakers of Christ's sufferings: that when his glory shall be revealed, ye may be glad also with exceeding joy.*

In this life we live, we must suffer sometimes. We must go through heartache, but once we see Christ in all His glory, hey, no more suffering, no more problems. Only joy. Peter said with Jude, *"exceeding joy."* That's far more joy than you and I could ever imagine. What an awesome God we serve.

Jude 25-To the only wise God our Savior, be glory and majesty, dominion and power, both now and ever. Amen.

To the only wise- I am reminded of a verse in Proverbs concerning wisdom and who it is that obtains all wisdom. Proverbs 3:9-*The LORD by wisdom hath founded the earth; by understanding hath he established the heavens.* No man could ever speak and bring to life a world, a solar system, or a person into being. No, only God, the all wise Potentate.

Also, Solomon said of God; 21:30-*There is no wisdom nor understanding nor counsel against the LORD.* Mankind throughout the ages have tried to explain away God. They've used science, history, deceit and just plain lies. But God remains true, His way is forever.

David said of God; Psalms 147:5-*Great is our Lord, and of great power: his understanding is infinite.* Jude said, *"to the only wise"* and how true a statement. David affirms this statement hundreds of years before Jude was ever alive. God's understanding is infinite.

That word <u>infinite</u> means *without limits.* There is no limit to the knowledge of God. What we often ponder on, God knew before we were ever created.

God our Savior- Isaiah said in chapter 12:2-*Behold, God is my salvation; I will trust, and not be afraid: for the Lord Jehovah is my strength and my song; he also is become my salvation.* We often forget that the only hope we have in this life and in the next is that God is our Savior. Never forget the truth spoken here in this verse. Lastly Jude ended his letter with;

Be glory and majesty, dominion and power, both now and ever. Amen- Allow me to give you the meaning of the following words;

1. <u>Glory-</u>*honor, renounce; glory, and especially divine quality, the unspoken manifestation of God, splendor.*
2. <u>Majesty-</u> *Devine greatness.*
3. <u>Dominion-</u> *strength, and power.*
4. <u>Power-</u> *authority.*

Christ when He prayed, giving the disciples an example of prayer, said the following in Matthew 6:13-*And lead us not into temptation, but deliver us from evil; for thine is the kingdom, and the power, and the glory, for ever. Amen.*

I believe that He spoke this while illustrating to us how to pray, so that we would always remember that God should receive the proper glory from his children. God is Ruler over His creation. Though Satan may be a prince down here, he is still, and will always be, subject to God. Also, God is the Final Authority, He has all power.

If we constantly remembered these attributes of God, we wouldn't waver as often as we do during our battles. We wouldn't be so quick to stumble in our faith. Jude, following the example of Christ, wanted to also remind us of the greatness of our God.

He spent the greater portion of his letter telling us and warning us about apostasy. He wanted to remind us that, hey, everything is going to be ok, just keep Christ first in your life. What a wonderful ending to a powerful letter from the half-brother of our Lord and Savior Jesus Christ. I truly hope that you received strength, knowledge and a blessing from this study in the book of Jude.

****

Please be sure to rate and review this book on Amazon. Also, check out the Biblical Teaching Podcast available on your mobile device or desk top through the device's podcast app. The Biblical Teaching Podcast is a ministry that teaches the Bible verse by verse, helping Christians to have a better understanding of the Word of God.

My next commentary will be on the book of 1 Corinthians and should be available sometime in mid-2018.

Made in the USA
Columbia, SC
06 October 2021